Buying a Manufactured Home

Buying a Manufactured Home

FAMILY ROOM
18'-0" X 12'-10"

How to Get the Most Bang for Your Buck in Today's Housing Market

PASS-THRU

ARCHWAY

KITCHEN

ISLAND

MORNING
ROOM
7'-9" X 12'-4"

OPT.
HALF ROUND
WINDOW

PANTRY

ARCHWAY

Kevin Burnside

LIVING ROOM
18'-10" X 12'-10"

HOME RESOURCES books
are published by
Van der Plas Publications – San Francisco

Published by
Van der Plas Publications
1282 7th Avenue
San Francisco, CA 94122, U.S.A.
E-mail: rob@vanderplas.net
Website: http://www.vanderplas.net

Cover design
Kent Lytle, Lytle Design, Alameda CA

Cover photographs
Courtesy Wick Building Systems, Inc., Marshfield, WI

Publisher's Cataloging-in-Publication Data
Burnside, Kevin. Buying a Manufactured Home: How to Get the Most Bang
for Your Buck in Today's Housing Market. II / Kevin Burnside.
Bibliography: p. cm. Includes index.
ISBN 1-892495-00-7
1. House buying–manuals and handbooks. 2. Manufactured Housing. 3. Mobile
Homes. I. Title. II. Title: How to Get the Most Bang for Your Buck in Today's
Housing Market.
Library of Congress Catalog Card Number 99-70799

To Jeri, for her faithful companionship,
and Eloise Dielman for her time, effort, and hard work.
Thanks for your faith in me.

About the Author:

Kevin Burnside first became interested in manufactured housing in 1991, while working in real estate. He soon became the top producing salesman for one of the largest Fleetwood dealers in the country, and went on to become sales coordinator for a nationwide manufacturer.

His accomplishments include setting up a customer-friendly sales process along with finance and behavior-style training.

His experience affords him keen insights into all aspects of manufactured housing, including selection, contract negotiation, financing, and set-up.

Kevin lives with his family in Idaho.

Table of Contents

1.

Introduction

MANUFACTURED housing is claiming an increasingly significant share of the housing market in North America. According to Dr. Carol Meeks, author of *Manufactured Home Life Study*, published in 1995, 18 million people in the U.S., or 7% of the population live in 7.3 million manufactured homes, and their share is increasing every year. Still called "mobile homes" by many, these factory-built houses are a far cry from the trailer homes of yore.

The German architect Walter Gropius was perhaps the first one to propose factory-built housing as early as 1910. He wanted to bring his idea to the United States, but financial problems, labor resistance, and building codes thwarted his attempts. After World War II, however, his dream came true—to an extent. He did not quite have the idea of towing oversized loads on the highways. His dream was further distorted by those wanting to circumvent building codes, work rules, and vested interests. The manufactured home industry has responded to a fundamental social need, affordable housing, by marketing a commodity.

Thank goodness, today's manufactured homes are far better than the original variety. But, because the industry is a business that markets a commodity, you must realize its interests are not always yours.

The purpose of this book is to help you arm yourself with knowledge, so you won't be "eaten alive" by greedy salespeople and dealers, poor service, and uncaring contractors. The more time I worked in the business, the more I saw that these unscrupulous practices were not exclusive to just my little corner, but were industry-wide. It includes both the attitude of dealers toward their customers and that of manufacturers toward retailers.

I found after a few years that not only was the price of manufactured homes going up considerably, but the stereotypical "trailer" buyer had become not so typical. I myself grew up in a 1965 10 x 50 Kit trailer. We were not rich but had enough money to put food on the table. I don't recall any of our neighbors having more than a modest income either.

As site-built homes increase in cost, more well-to-do folks are taking notice of factory-built homes due to their vast improvements and design. Twenty, thirty years ago, "trailers" were an affordable means of shelter for people with meager to modest incomes. Today, people with meager to modest incomes still have this opportunity to buy a home, but some of the industry's offerings are substantial enough to appeal to others as well.

Today the industry of manufactured homes is different. All levels of income have choices and need to know how and where to go for financing, contractors, and finding the best brands and dealers.

My intention with this book is to help you save time, money, and piece of mind. Buying a home, whether manufactured or site-built, can be a taxing project. It's probably the single largest purchase you will make in your life. The book will help you deal with the process.

Fig. 1.1 The low end of manufactured housing: a two-bedroom single-wide on a simple cinder block foundation. Note the skirting to hide the gap under the home.

Although I have some harsh words for some of the practices that are only too common in this business, I am not out to "get" the industry.

My hope is that all those in the industry who read these pages walk away with perhaps a bit more information regarding what it is like to go through the buying process and realize the stress and worry that home buyers experience.

Also, I'd like to address the price issue. The section of the book devoted to negotiation and how to establish the least amount of profit a dealer is willing to take is not there because I feel the dealer doesn't deserve to make a profit, but simply to level the playing field.

My concerns lie with the dealerships, and the businesses that own several dealerships, with in-house financing and insurance divisions. Each of these areas should be profitable, but why max out people's monthly payments? Why charge interest rates that are too high? Why use covert sales tactics and withhold pertinent information from those who need it? Other major points of frustration I have are the following:

◻ Manufacturers and dealers fighting over who is responsible for different warranty areas of the home.

◻ Poorly trained sales people and dealers not giving honest information, trying to gouge home buyers and not offering option—financing options, insurance options, contractor options, etc.

Fig. 1.2. By no means the high end of modern manufactured housing, but a lot more residential-looking, this double-wide with attached garage

◻ Manufacturers and retailers still peddling "down and dirty trailers," that is, homes built to the absolute minimum of the HUD code.

◻ Insufficient regulation and enforcement of laws governing set-up and the licensing of set-up crews.

I do not want to put down hard working salespeople trying to make a living. I was one. Not all salespeople work hard and not all care about you, but most want to see the people who do business with them happy. The nature of sales is stressful. Sell something or get fired. Too many salespeople operate in survival mode and see a potential sale as just that: a sale. They forget that the sale has a name and a life attached to it.

This survival mode is a natural outcome of the sales profession and is exacerbated by the dealerships the salespeople work for. Instead of general managers and sales managers demanding a monthly and yearly quota from each salesperson, why not train and give the tools to each salesperson to actually help every customer that walks through the door accomplish home ownership. That would mean helping the buyer obtain the best financing and payment terms and select the right options, and ensuring thorough follow-through once the homeowner has taken possession of the house. Doesn't that sound like a good company mission statement?

The majority of my time in the business was spent at one of the better dealers, who was sincere about customer satisfaction, and I have

Fig. 1.3. The hillside location suggested the use of a basement and upper-story deck on this large manufactured home.

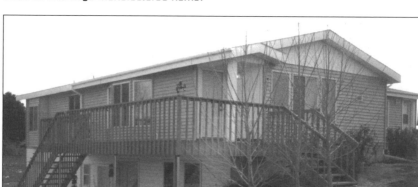

Table 0.1. U.S. Home sales development since 1980 (Manufactured home shipments and single-family housing starts and homes sold)

Year	Manufactured Home Shipments	New Single Fam. starts	Manufactured Homes as % of total starts	New Single Fam. sold	Manufactured Homes as % of New homes sold
1980	221,091	852,200	20.6%	545,000	28.9%
1981	240,313	705,400	25.4%	436,000	35.5%
1982	238,808	662,600	26.5%	412,000	36.7%
3983	295,079	1,067,600	21.7%	623,000	32.1%
1984	294,993	1,084,200	21.4%	639,000	31.6%
1985	283,489	1,072,400	20.9%	688,000	29.2%
1986	244,660	1,179,400	17.2%	750,000	24.6%
1987	232,598	1,146,400	16.9%	671,000	25.7%
1988	210,429	1,081,300	16.8%	676,000	24.4%
1989	198,254	1,003,300	16.5%	650, 000	23.4%
1990	188,172	894,800	17.4%	534,000	26.1%
1991	170,713	840,400	16.9%	507,000	25.2%
1992	210,787	1,030,100	17.0%	610,000	25.7%
1993	254,276	1,125,600	18.4%	666,000	27.6%
1994	303, 932	1,198,400	20.2%	670,000	31.2%
1995	339,601	1,076,300	24.0%	667,000	33.7%
1996	363,411	1,160,900	23.8%	758,000	32.4%
1997	353,377	1,133,500	23.87	801,000	30.6%

Notes:

New Single Family housing starts are new site-built homes that were constructed during the year.

New Single Family homes sold are those site-built homes that actually sold out of the ones built.

been employed by a large corporation that didn't. I have also spent time at the factory level, so I do have the full picture for you to view in these pages. I suggest you visit the factory that builds the brand of home you are interested in purchasing. Take the book with you and take thorough notes. You will learn much more than through talking to salespeople.

My experience has been in the Pacific Northwest. You may have to adapt some of the information I provide to the part of the country where you live. For example, the Super Good Cents program for energy-efficient homes in the Northwest may have a different name where you live, or it may not exist at all.

The way you option your home and how it is set up will also vary. Many manufactured homes are set on solid poured foundations in the Northwest, much more often than, for instance, in the Southeast. Your insulation needs will vary, siding needs will vary, and even air conditioner needs will differ from region to region.

The one constant, however, is that dealers want maximum profit from you.

Read this before you begin your home buying process, and don't skip anything. A project this big won't always have an exact sequence, and glitches sometimes occur. Building permit hold-ups, undependable contractors, drawn-out financing, and a host of other variables can get in the way. But this information will give you the power to negotiate for all aspects of your purchase and financing. You'll know how to get the best home and how to work with contractors.

If you have been through this process before, combine what you've learned from your own experience with the information in this book, and your project will go much smoother, because you will be well prepared. Happy home hunting!

Looking at Manufactured Homes

SO YOU'RE in the market for a new home. How about looking into a manufactured home? Yes, a "trailer." Before you wrinkle your nose and shudder, drive by a dealership and take a look. These aren't trailers anymore, a fact recognized by the new home industry. In fact, in the last decade, even financial institutions have stepped up to the plate and now offer "site-built" financing for manufactured homes.

Today's Manufactured Homes

Manufacturers of "mobile homes" have realized that all types of potential home buyers would be interested in their homes if they didn't look like trailers with aluminum siding. Couple that with the indisputable fact that homes built on-site are astronomically expensive and can take months to build. During the 1980s, as the cost of lumber began to creep higher and higher, more potential homeowners were stopped from achieving their goal of owning a "stick-built" house.

Manufacturers in different parts of the country started producing homes that met or surpassed the energy efficiency standards of utility companies and new codes instituted for quality control.

The new improvements in manufactured homes included 2 x 6 inch exterior walls, vinyl-clad dual pane windows, insulation with high R-values, and hardboard siding. Even seasoned home buyers are taking note—imagine a house with all this "site-built" material for only $30.00 per square foot. But how much "site-built" is really built in one of these new "trailers"—20%, 40%, or 80%? What are the components made of and where do they come from?

Until 1976, the "trailer" industry built just that, trailers. Mobile homes varied in size from single-section measuring 8 x 40, 10 x 50, 10 x 55 and 12 x 60 feet to double-section homes that were 18 x 40 and 20 x 50 feet, among others. These homes had tail lights and hitches, used to move the home, that were never removed and quite frequently became the base of a flower box.

Manufacturers did not have to comply with strict building codes or minimum standards. A trailer was typically built on two I-beams. The floor was built on top of them, and then walls and roofing were added. That sounds pretty slick at first, but what in the world was the floor made of? The exterior walls were often built with 1 x 2s, with the same aluminum siding used in R.V. construction. The roof was metal, with seams that needed caulking every fall, and the ceiling always leaked and was stained where the swamp cooler sat.

Windows were typically the famous roll out, three-tier jobs that seemed to be open even when they were closed. The interior walls were maybe one inch thick and had no sound insulation (nor was there much insulation in exterior walls, the floor, or the roof cavity).

Fig. 2.1. A larger manufactured home with attached garage.

The ceiling was barely seven feet from the floor, and the appliances, sinks, and fixtures were undersized, like something from the land of Lilliput.

The house was set on cinder blocks and the gap was hidden with corrugated metal skirting.

The oil furnace always gave off fumes and never could keep up with the cold breeze that rushed through the house.

As you can tell, I turned this description personal because I grew up in a 1965 model single-wide. It was like living in an oversized hallway; perhaps you know what I'm talking about. Thank goodness mobile homes have improved a lot since those days.

However, there are things consumers should be aware of—quality of construction, financing, real estate concerns, installation matters, and of course, price.

Everything presented to you here is a matter of fact. Manufactured homes are a great way to go in meeting your housing needs, but the industry is still growing and maturing. While retailers and manufacturers alike are prospering, that should not be at the buyer's expense.

Frame Construction

The one thing that has been a constant in the construction of factory-built housing (manufactured homes) is the steel I-beam chassis on which the home is built. Whether it is a single-section, double-section, or triple-

Fig. 2.2. Floor plan of a modest double-wide home with 2 bedrooms.

section home, each section has two I-beams running the full length. The size of these I-beams can vary from 8 to 12 inches, depending on the length and weight of the home. These steel beams (or "chassis system") serve two purposes. One is that they are the support of the floor system. The wood floor system is attached to the I-beams. They give the home torsional stiffness (resistance against twisting) while allowing appropriate "give" during transport from the factory to the home's destination.

The second reason steel I-beams are used is quite simple: there has to be a place to attach the axles and wheels to move the home from the factory to your site. You might say the steel I-beam chassis is integrated into the entire floor system.

I have had people want to set their manufactured homes on a basements and then remove the I-beams. Not only is this against federal law, but as any structural engineer can tell you, there would be no practical way to set the home on the basement in accordance with the manufacturers specifications. Plus, you can kiss your warranty good-bye.

Fig. 2.3. From the ground up: Manufactured homes are built on a steel chassis made up of I-beams, shown here with the floor joists installed. Each section has its own chassis, and finally the sections are joined at the "marriage line."

Types of Factory-Built Homes

Sizes of manufactured homes vary from just under 1,000 square feet clear up to 2,500 plus. There should be enough choices to fit everyone's needs. On these pages, you will find some examples of popular floor plans. It is possible to modify floor plans to suit, but the factory will charge the dealer. The dealer will in turn charge you, the buyer.

As you will see, floor plans and the quality of manufactured housing have come a long way. The bigger double and triple sections home plans will rival any "site-built", home.

Here is a brief list of the various types of manufactured homes that are available today, and the designations used for them, as defined by the Manufactured Housing Institute.

Several different types of structures are built in the factory and designed for long-term residential use. In the case of manufactured and modular homes, units are built in a factory, transported to the site and installed. In panelized and pre-cut homes, essentially flat units (factory-built panels or factory-cut building material) are transported to the site, where they are assembled.

Manufactured Home	A home built entirely in the factory under a federal building code administered by the Department of Housing and Urban Development (HUD). The Federal Manufactured Home Construction and Safety Standards (the HUD Code) went into effect

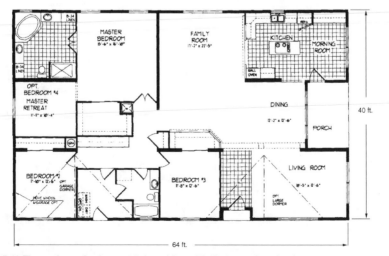

Fig. 2.4 Floor plan of a large triple-wide with three or four bedrooms.

June 15, 1976. Manufactured homes may be single- or multi-section and are transported to the site and installed. The federal standards regulate manufactured housing design and construction, strength and durability, transportability, fire resistance, energy efficiency, and quality. The HUD Code also sets performance standards for heating, plumbing, air conditioning, thermal and electrical systems. It is the only national building code.

Mobile Home

This is the term used for homes built prior to June 15, 1976, when the HUD Code went into effect. In many cases, particularly in North Carolina, these homes were built to voluntary industry standards.

Modular Home

These factory-built homes are built to the state, local or regional code where the home will be located. Multi-section units are transported to the site and installed.

Fig. 2.5. This is the next stage, when the floor decking is installed on the floor joists.

Panelized Home   Factory-built homes in which panels—a whole wall with windows, doors, wiring, and outside siding—are transported to the site and assembled. The homes must meet state or local building codes where they are sited.

Pre-Cut Home   Factory-built housing in which building materials are factory-cut to design specifications, transported to the site, and assembled. Pre-cut homes include kit, log, and dome homes. These homes must meet local or state building codes.

About HUD and Codes

In 1974, the U.S. Department of Housing and Urban Development (HUD) was designated as the agency to oversee the Federal Manufactured Housing Program. The area within HUD responsibility for the oversight function is the Office of Consumer and Regulatory Affairs, Manufactured Housing and Standards Division.

Fig. 2.6. Plumbing is installed and the floors and walls are insulated.

A manufactured home (formerly "mobile home" is built to the Manufactured Home Construction and Safety Standards ("HUD Code") and displays a red certification label on the exterior of each section.

Most states have a State Administrative Agency (SAA) that administers the HUD Program in that state.

The Uniform Building Code (UBC) is a set of requirements that apply to the construction of homes and is adopted by most states and counties. The UBC is stricter than the HUD Code regarding certain aspects of building.

The Way It's Built

Typically, factories are mere assembly lines with a group of workers doing the same function day in and day out. The home or section is pulled down the "line" and stopped for a specified amount of time. The line is moved again at the sound of a long whistle and flashing lights. Each stage of building is to be complete at each stop (this doesn't always

Fig. 2.7. A wall section is craned over to the assembly line.

happen, but for the most part, factories are fairly efficient and not much overlap occurs.

Once the floor system has been completed, the next step involves completing the plumbing and heating systems. The assembly line rolls on to the next stage, where the linoleum is laid the whole width of the section and tacked down in the bathroom and kitchen areas. Most manufacturers do not use glue. Then it's time to set the walls on the floor system. The walls are constructed in a different part of the plant and craned over to the "line." All four exterior walls are screwed into the floor and the interior walls are added.

All the cabinetry is installed, along with sinks and fixtures. Different factories will add these smaller items at different stages.

The ceiling will be next, and like the walls, it is built at a different location in the plant and craned over to the line, where it is lowered and secured to the tops of the walls. In many cases, the sheetrock has already been textured.

At this stage, for double- and triple-section homes, some manufacturers will temporarily join the sections together to make sure the interior walls line up as well as any "crossover connections" that

Fig. 2.8. A view of the roof trusses before the roof decking is installed on it.

need to be made: for electrical or plumbing connections. Not all factories do this step, but it seems to save many problems later.

Now that the sections have been joined and the roof installed, much more begins to happen. The roofers hop to and begin laying shingles. Drywallers begin to hang sheetrock in the home. Tile counter edges are installed and other detail work is done.

Next, the crew arrives to put protective plastic over sensitive areas (sinks, fixtures, cabinets, electric panel boxes, etc.) to protect them from the rather messy process of spraying on the texture. This is the "mud" that goes on to the walls and ceilings of homes on top of the sheetrock. The paint is usually mixed with the "mud" and applied at the same time.

You'll notice that since the ceilings are textured separate from the walls, rarely will you get matching texture application from wall to ceiling. There may be some manufacturers that are beginning to apply texture at the same time to walls and ceilings, but you will have to check.

Next, windows are installed and other detail work on the exterior is carried out. The sections are separated and the texture applicators step in for their part. During completion of the texture, the exterior of the house gets painted if the home has hardboard siding.

Fig. 2.9. Roofing shingles are applied to the roof.

Unfortunately, most manufactured homes are not painted as well as they should, and most manufacturers apply only a single coat of paint, whereas they should really use a primer first. If the home is to have vinyl or cement lap siding, it is applied at this stage. Hopefully, the manufacturer first applies some type of backer to attach the vinyl.

Shutters, window trim, fancy columns for the exterior front of the home, and light fixtures come next in the process.

The home is near completion, and quality control should be going through each section looking for defects before the home leaves the factory. Many times, however, defects get fixed in the field. That is, at your site.

Once the home is done, it is pulled from the factory to a staging area where it should be system-checked. Systems such as electrical and plumbing are checked. Natural gas systems are checked for leaks. Finally a red HUD tag is attached to the back of each section, showing that it has passed inspection. Then the home is taken to the site.

If it is a multi-section home, it is pushed and pulled together at the "mating" or "marriage" line. Ten- or twelve-inch-long bolts are used to secure the roof ridge and floor, while smaller lag bolts are used in the walls. Hopefully, the set-up crew has put some kind of insulation between the marriage lines.

Next, the dealer begins sending in all the subcontractors to do the necessary finish work prior to the buyer's "move in."

Fig. 2.10. Corner of a house before the siding is installed on the end wall. This one is being finished at the installation site.

This is a general sequence, subject to change due to individual order variations. With all the factories around the country, some will have deviations. For instance, some builders will put the axles and tires on the chassis after the house is completed, rather than putting them on the chassis first. Some factories will have a chain-driven assembly line that moves the homes smoothly and keeps them level, whereas others may hook the home to a forklift and move it to the next stage. For some factories, many stages of building go on outside, exposed to the weather, and some manufacturers even store their building material outside because their factory is too small for storage.

3.

Home Hunting

THESE DAYS, it is not uncommon to visit a manufactured home dealership and see a $128,000 triple-wide home. What happened to $30 per square foot? Where has the idea gone of offering everyone the chance to become a homeowner of a quality home? What, if anything, have many manufacturers and dealers done to combat the high cost of lumber, materials and labor?

While I'd like to reassure you, I would suggest that potential buyers read each of the following chapters carefully, because

Fig. 3.1. Although quite large, this is still a rather modest double-wide, sitting on a poured concrete foundation, waiting for move-in.

unfortunately many manufacturers and dealers now leave some materials out to bring you in.

As with many quickly growing industries, the manufactured housing industry is experiencing growing pains. These come in a variety of forms, including sales centers that are unprofessional and use dishonest, high-pressure sales tactics. They have high turnover of sales personnel and no follow-through after sales. Manufacturers pressure the dealers to buy a certain number of homes. If the dealer can't meet the expected quota, he or she faces losing that brand and holdback money.

Nevertheless, you would think that salespeople and owners of dealerships would understand that buying a home is the single largest purchase a family will make, and that the used car sales approach should be thrown out. Again, because of the enormous explosion in popularity

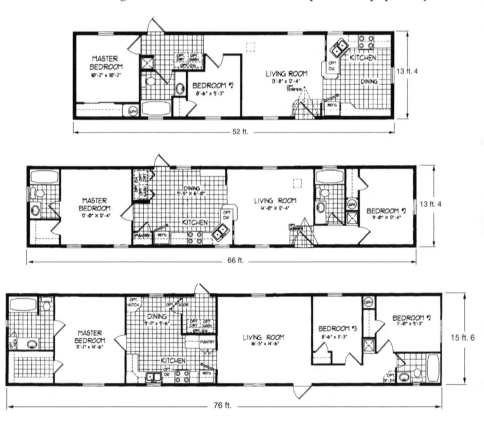

Fig. 3.2 Three single-wide floor plans. From top to bottom a two-bed, one-bath 693 sq. ft. home; a two-bed, two-bath 880 sq. ft. home, and a three-bed, two-bath 1178 sq. ft. model that measures 15 ft. 6 by 76 ft—that's about as big as any single-wide on the market today.

of manufactured homes, competition has become fierce and territorial. Thus, as a potential buyer, you need to be on your guard: Your pocketbook is their target.

Whether you are a first-time home buyer, an empty nester, or a retiree, a manufactured home will work for you, but first you need to know these critical items:

1. Which dealer is most reputable?

2. What brand is best?

3. How is the home constructed?

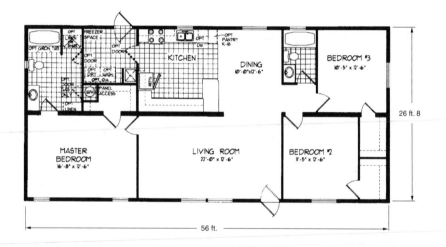

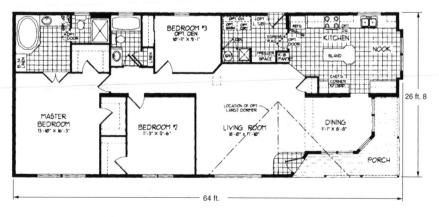

Fig. 3.3. Two 3-bedroom double-wides, with 1,493 and 1,707 sq. ft. respectively.

4.   What type of components are in the home?

5.   What are the finance options?

6.   Who will do the improvements on the property?

7.   Who has the best prices?

8.   What options and upgrades should you order with the house?

9.   What do you need to know about the contract?

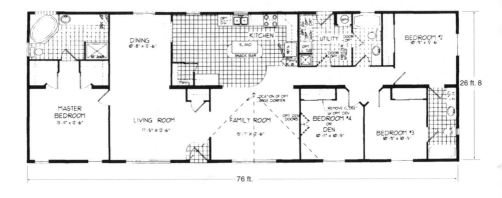

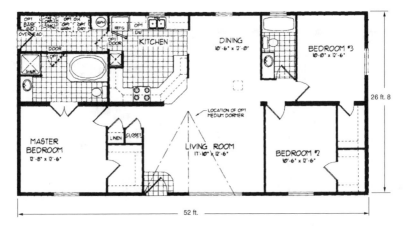

Fig. 3.4. Two double-wides. Top, a 4-bed, 3-bath model with 2,027 sq. ft.; below, a compact 1,387 sq. ft. 3-bed, 2-bath model.

10. How can you control the sales process?

11. Is a "factory direct" dealership going to sell you a home for less?

12. How do you ensure service after the sale?

Knowledge is power. As you read these pages, mentally prepare yourself to be in control. You are not buying a home to make friends with a salesperson. Think about that 30-year mortgage you are taking on. Don't you deserve the best home and service for your hard-earned money?

Here is a list of things you need to consider about each manufactured home you look at:

Roof	How are the shingles rated—20, 25, or 30 years? What is the warranty? Are the shingles held down with nails or staples? If nails, how many per shingle? How thick is the roof decking that the shingles are attached to? Are the shingles laid correctly, with an offset pattern or are they lined up? Is roof felt used?
Trusses and eaves	What size are the trusses and how far apart are they? How wide are the eaves, front, back, and ends? Is there ventilation under the eaves to allow the attic cavity to breathe? What kind of insulation is in the attic cavity? What is the R-value?

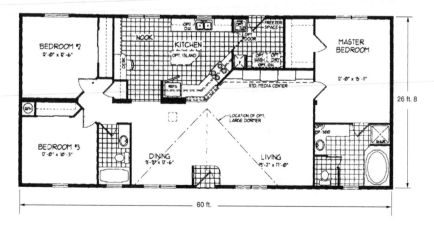

Fig. 3.5. A 1,600 sq. ft. 3-bed, 2-bath model

Siding

If hardboard siding is used, what is it made of, and what is the warranty? Is it attached to a backer? If vinyl siding is used, is there a backer behind it that it is attached to? What kind of paint has been applied? What is the warranty on the vinyl siding? Are the eaves and fascia hardboard even though the siding is vinyl? Is there Tyvek house wrap under the siding? What type of shutters come with the vinyl siding?

Exterior Walls

Are the exterior walls 2 x 6, 16 inches on center? What is the R-value of the insulation in the exterior walls? Is the lumber in the house kiln dried? Is the bottom plate, or sole plate, of the exterior wall a 2 x 6 or a 1 x 4?

Floors

What size are the floor joists—2 x 6 or 2 x 8? How far apart are they? Which direction do they run, longitudinally or transverse? How thick is the floor decking? What is it made of and how is it

Fig. 3.6. A 2,000 sq. ft. 3-bed, 2-bath triple-wide. Not necessarily bigger, but more residential-looking than a double-wide.

applied—staples, screws, or nails? Is glue used in conjunction with the fastening method? What is the R-value of the insulation in the floor?

Windows   What is the brand of the windows? Are they vinyl-clad, dual pane windows with low-E glass? (Don't be concerned with argon gas-filled windows—the gas seeps out in a few years.)

Deck and entry   If your house has a built-on wood deck, is it weather sealed?

Recessed entry   If your house has a recessed entry, how "deep" is it? What's under that indoor-outdoor carpet—marine plywood or regular floor decking?

Hitch   Is the hitch removable?

Interior   How thick is the sheetrock on the ceiling and the walls? How is it applied, with drywall screws or is it "foamed" on?

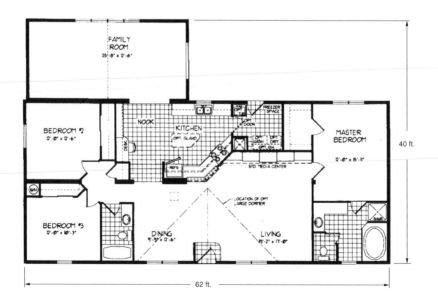

Fig. 3.7. A 1,956 sq. ft. L-shaped triple-wide with three bedrooms and two baths.

Is the texture orange-peel or knockdown? Does the ceiling texture match the wall texture? Where the ceiling meets the top of the wall, is the joint filled with caulking or is it taped? What kind of interior paint is used, flat or semi-gloss?

Are the window sills taped and textured or particle board wrapped with white vinyl? Are the mini blinds plastic or metal? Do the valances have a backing?

Carpet

Best advice: Don't take any carpet. Have the dealer omit it because it's all low- quality "trailer" carpet. Have the dealer give you the somewhat meager credit, find out how many square yards are in the house, and pick out good carpet at a carpet store. Just add the price of the carpet to the purchase contract for the house.

Air circulation and ventilation

What does the internal air exchange system consist of? Is it passive or mechanical?

Doors

What kind of hinges are on the interior doors, mortised or butterfly? (Butterfly hinges tend to "let go" quickly.)

Should the front door or back door have a window in it? Glass is popular, but there may be a safety issue involved. Also the white plastic that borders the glass will turn bright yellow after it is exposed to the sun (in 2 or 3 months).

Are the front and rear doors steel and insulated? How wide are they?

How wide are the interior doorways? Are the doorknobs metal or plastic? Are the doors full length or two inches off the floor?

Bathrooms and plumbing

Are the bathroom sinks plastic, porcelain, or vitreous china? Are the faucets plastic or metal? Are the tubs plastic or one-piece fiberglass? Do the bathrooms come with a towel bar and toilet paper holder? Is there a tile back-splash in the kitchen and baths? Are there shut-off valves under the sinks and behind the toilets? Is there a medicine cabinet? How about strip lighting over the bathroom sink? GFI (ground-fault interrupt electric outlets) in baths and kitchen? What kind of floor covering is used in the bathroom?

Kitchen

Are cabinets and cabinet doors wood or particle board?

Are the drawer fronts and cabinet doors wood, whereas the base cabinet is particle board wrapped in a fake wood-look vinyl? What kind of Formica is in the home, and where are the seams located (for instance, seams near the sink shelves? How deep is the sink in the kitchen, 6 inches or 8 inches? Is it stainless steel or porcelain? Does the range hood have a light and a fan? What brands of appliances come with the house? Does it have a shelf or cabinets for laundry storage?

Is there an outlet for a freezer?

What brand and quality of sheet vinyl ("linoleum") is on the floor in the kitchen and utility area?

Skylights

Skylights are nice, but they let in a lot of heat during the summer, and often they will eventually leak.

4.

Financing: Shop for Money First

READ THIS section slowly and carefully. Let its message soak into your skin and course through your veins. Why? Every dealer is out to make as much profit from you as possible, not only by asking for the highest possible purchase price, but through financing as well. Manufactured home dealers get a "kickback" at the end of the year from "in house" lenders. This kickback, or rebate, is one to two percent of every "deal" the dealership gets financed.

But first, let me give you some inside information on cash buyers versus financing. To the dealer, it's all the same. It doesn't matter to him whether you give him the money or the bank does. So paying cash does not guarantee a big discount, even if the dealer says something to that effect.

How much you pay for the money the bank lends you can make a huge difference to your final payments and the total sum you end up paying for your home over the years. To show you what's involved, we'll follow an imaginary couple, Tara and Travis, around as they shop for a home.

A Scenario For Paying Too Much

Travis and Tara are first-time home buyers with good credit. They want to buy land and a new home for their new addition—their first child. They are good, dependable renters who always pay the rent on time and have lived in the community for many years. They have also managed to save a hefty down payment.

One Sunday they stop at a dealership with a big, bright sign in front that reads: "One stop shopping! We finance and insure right here!" Travis and Tara are fond of convenience, so they stop for a look. The salesman tells Travis and Tara that the dealership obtains financing and can provide homeowners' insurance as required by all lenders. Sounds good, doesn't it? Convenience is a wonderful thing. Now let's see what the convenience of one-stop shopping is going to cost Travis and Tara.

A. Home:

Purchase price of home	$50,000.00
Air conditioner	$1,900.00
Subtotal	$51,900.00
Tax @ 5%	$2,595.00
House total	**$54,495.00**

B. Site:

Price of land	$25,000.00
Foundation, well, power, septic	$14,000.00
Site total	**$39,000.00**
Total package price	**$93,495.00**

The finance companies that the dealership uses, work on a few simple premises: low down payment, high interest rates. Watch carefully:

Total land-home package price $93,495.00

Less 5% down payment. . . . . − $4,674.75

Amount to finance **$88,820.25**

Typical finance company interest rate: 9.75%

If Travis and Tara finance $88,829.25 for 30 years at 9.75%, their monthly payment is $763.10, not including tax and insurance. A safe figure to add is $150.00 per month to cover these items.

Monthly total: **$913.10**

The dealer gets a kickback of about $1,300.00 from the lender.

How to Get a Better Deal

If, instead, Travis and Tara had gone to a bank, a credit union, or a mortgage broker first, they may have found they qualified for an 8% interest rate. If we recalculate costs, we discover they could have had a better deal.

Total land-home package price $93,497.00

10% down payment . . . . − $9,349.70

Amount to finance. $84,147.30

Financing $84,147.30 for 30 years at 8.00%, they would have a monthly payment of $617.45. Again, they would still have to budget the additional $150 per month to cover insurance and taxes, of course.

Monthly total **$767.17**

Assuming they take the full 30 years to pay off their mortgage, they will pay a total of $185,895,75 in interest, if they finance with the dealership. If instead they finance with the 8% mortgage for 30 years, their total will be only $138,134.70. That's a $47,000 difference.

Isn't it worth one hour of your time to go to a bank to save $47,000? Isn't it worth one hour of your time to change your monthly payment from $913 to $767 on the same loan?

The next thing that went wrong for Travis and Tara is that they fell for the car dealership trick: "What kind of monthly payment are you looking for?" Answering that makes the customer an easy prey for a salesman.

Why is the payment approach flawed? The negotiation is based on a figure that came out of nowhere and is not based on the price of a house. Salespeople love this. If you, the buyer, don't have a payment in mind before doing your finance homework, the sales person will find a house for you that could have been financed for much less—I guarantee it.

Dealers also prefer to finance home buyers with their lenders because the dealer gets "funded" by the lender before your house is delivered to your site. The dealer achieves total control and you are left to his whim. A very good reason to obtain financing somewhere else.

A Road Map to Better Financing

Here's a road map of a better route to financing. By getting prequalified, you will know what payment you can afford and how much total you can borrow. I recommend visiting at least three sources to gather information. These sources can give you an estimate, and then give you an exact figure of the annualized percentage rate (APR) which you qualify for, as well as how much money you can borrow. Don't be shy about asking questions. Lending money is what keeps lenders in business.

Terms of the Loan

Should you finance for 30 years or 15 years? The answer to this question depends on your comfort level and what you have qualified for. Here's an example:

15 year loan for $80,000.00

Interest 8%

Monthly payment $765.52

30 year loan for $80,000.00

Interest	8%
Monthly payment	$587.01
Monthly difference	**$177.51**

If you are comfortable with $177.51 more a month to own your home in 15 years instead of in 30 years, then do it. If not, take a 30-year mortgage and make just one extra payment a year. By making this one extra payment per year, you will turn your 30-year mortgage into perhaps a 23-year mortgage. The banks usually don't like this bit of information publicized because they will make less money.

Variable Interest Rates

Variable interest rates that go up or down according to the prime lending rate can be a real advantage. Be careful, however, Depending upon the economy and the indicator your rate is tied to, your interest rate could go from 7% to 8% in two years. Can you afford $200.00 more per month? At the time of writing of this book, conforming rates are stable at 7% or so, which makes for a decent, consistent payment. You must choose which you are most comfortable with.

Graduated Interest Rates

Don't let dealerships hook you; that is, don't let them talk you into their financing with graduated rates and rate sales. Graduated rates work like a step ladder. The rate starts low and then year after year for the first three to five years, it increases incrementally. How does a starting rate of 8% sound? Pretty good, huh? However, a rate that starts at 8% and goes to 12% in 5 years does this to your monthly payment:

1st year:	$500.00
2nd year:	$547.00
3rd year:.	$592.00
4th year:.	$638.00
5th year and all following years:.	$684.00

When you look at it this way, it doesn't look so good, does it?

If you are a first-time home buyer and have found out you have good credit, you can qualify for a 3% down program through a reputable bank or mortgage broker, and qualify for the current conforming interest rates.

Let's explain the term "conforming," which you'll frequently hear as you are going through the financing process. Conforming loans are ones that meet all the lender's guidelines. An example would be a home buyer with "excellent type A" credit who meets all the other criteria set forth by the lender to obtain a mortgage to buy a home and/or land.

There are many lenders who will lend money to people with less than perfect, non-conforming, credit. That is, B, C, or D credit. These loans require a higher down payment and will have higher interest rates. However, in many cases, after just 24 to 36 months of making your mortgage payments on time and keeping up with any other payments, you may be able to finance at a low conforming interest rate.

Figuring What Your Payments Buy

Here is a chart to determine what a certain payment will buy in a lump sum of money.

Table 2.1: Monthly payments in $ per $1,000 borrowed

Term of loan	Percentage (APR)							
	6.0%	6.5%	7.0%	7.5%	8.0%	8.5%	9.0%	9.5%
15 years	84.38	87.11	89.88	91.70	95.56	98.47	101.42	107.46
20 years	71.64	74.56	77.53	80.56	83.64	86.78	89.97	106.50
25 years	64.43	67.53	70.68	73.90	77.18	80.52	83.92	90.87
30 years	59.95	63.21	66.53	69.92	73.38	76.89	80.46	87.75

Divide what you plan to pay per month by the payment per $1,000.00 borrowed from this table; then multiply by 10,000—(just move the decimal 4 places to the right).

Here's an example. Say you've decided to spend $500 per month for 30 years at 8.5% interest.

1. Go to the column and find the length of the term; then find the interest rate, and find 76.89 where they intersect.

2. $500.0 divided by 76.89 equals 6.5028. (If your calculator does not carry out past 6.50, just add two zeroes to the figure: 65,000.)

3. Move the decimal 4 places to the right: $500 per month will buy you $65,027.96.

By knowing how to use this chart, you will know more about financing than most salespeople know. Let's try another one: $600.00 monthly payment for 25 years at 8%

1. From the table, read off 77.18

2. $600.00 divided by 77.18 equals 7.7740347.

3. Move the decimal 4 places to the right = $77,740.35

It's vital to know and understand that a monthly payment "buys" a lump sum of cash. Once you are qualified at your local bank, and you know what you can spend, and more importantly, how much you are comfortable spending per month, you won't have to rely on a salesperson to calculate amounts for you.

Once you are comfortable calculating from this chart, sit down and think about how much house and money you need. My suggestion is to take what you want to spend a month on your home and add all other debt to it. Add only the minimum monthly payments to the house payment. Don't count utility bills, food, etc. Just VISA, MasterCard, child support, car payments, etc. Here's an example:

House payment	$500
Car payment and furniture	$350
Total	**$850**

Divide $850 by your gross monthly income. Say you make $3,500.00 per month, total household income. Take $850 and divide by 3,500; that equals 0.24, or 24%. If the answer exceeds 36%, your house payment needs to be lower or you need to pay off some existing bills first. Ignore anything else a dealer may say. Their interest is in making the highest possible profit, not what's best for you.

Dealing with Points

A word about points. I don't recommend them. What points do is buy a lower interest rate. Generally one point (1 percent) of the amount you are financing will lower your interest rate by one quarter of a percent. It can be confusing and causes the closing costs of your loan to be higher. Manufactured home dealers love points because the finance companies they work with will actually add the cost of your points onto your loan amount. Isn't that a bit self-defeating? It doesn't make much sense to reduce your interest rate while at the same time increasing your loan amount, does it? Even points at a bank or credit union are something to avoid.

Mortgage Types Compared

The Mortgage Money Guide, provided by the Federal Trade Commission urges home buyers to use a comparison and quick check chart to determine which type of mortgage will work best for you.

30-Year Fixed Rate Mortgage

Fixed interest rate, long term (up to 30 years)

Pros: Offers stable payments and long-term tax advantages

Cons: Interest rate can be a bit higher than other kinds of financing.

15-Year Fixed Rate Mortgage

Fixed interest rate; may require a higher down payment than a 30-year mortgage.

Pros: Equity will be gained more quickly in your property and interest rates can be lower than with a 30-year mortgage

Cons: It requires higher monthly payments.

Adjustable Rate Mortgage

Interest rate changes over the life of the loan.

Pros: Beginning interest rate is below market. Rate caps can limit payment.

Cons: Payments can increase quickly.

Balloon Mortgage

Fixed rate, short term; the payments may cover interest only, with the loan amount due in full at a specified time.

Pros: Can offer low monthly payments

Cons: Chance of no equity until loan is paid in full.

Graduated Interest Rate or Payment Mortgage

Monthly payments rise gradually, then stabilize for the rest of the loan.

Pros: This loan can be easier to qualify for.

Cons: Your income must keep pace with the payment increase.

Shared Appreciation Mortgage

Below market rate and low monthly payments in exchange for a share of profits when property is sold.

Pros: Low rate, low payments.

Cons: If the property appreciates, the cost of the loan goes up. If the property depreciates, the projected increase in value may still be due.

The following chart shows the maximum monthly amount you can make for home payments and total monthly obligations depending on your annual income. No more than 28% of your gross monthly income (before taxes) should be used for mortgage payments (principal, interest, taxes, insurance, mortgage insurance). No more than 36% of your gross monthly income should be going toward your mortgage payment plus all other monthly obligations (car loan, credit cards, etc.).

Annual Income	Monthly mortgage payment	Monthly total credit obligations
$ 20,000.00	$ 467.00	$ 600.00
$ 30,000.00	$ 700.00	$ 900.00
$ 40,000.00	$ 933.00	$1,200.00
$ 50,000.00	$1,167.00	$1,500.00
$ 60,000.00	$1,400.00	$1,800.00
$ 70,000.00	$1,633.00	$2,100.00
$ 80,000.00	$1,867.00	$2,400.00
$ 90,000.00	$2,100.00	$2,700.00
$100,000.00	$2,333.00	$3,000.00
$130,000.00	$3,033.00	$3,900.00
$150,000.00	$3,500.00	$4,500.00

(Source: *Unraveling the Mortgage Loan Mystery*, Federal National Mortgage Association.)

Calculating Your Mortgage Payment

The following tables will tell you what the monthly payments will be for different interest rates and terms (principal and interest). For example, a monthly payment for a $60,000.00 30-year fixed loan at 8% would be $440.26. For amounts over $100,000.00, add two payments together that equal the numbers for the amount. Example: $125,000.00 loan, 8% interest, 30 years. First find the payment for $100,000.00. Then the payment for $25,000.00, and just add them together for the payment.

$100,000.00 payment $733.76

$ 25,000.00 payment $183.44

$125,000.00 payment . . . . $917..20

Monthly payment of principal and interest
6% Annual Percentage Rate

Amount of Loan	Term of mortgage				
	10 years	15 years	20 years	25 years	30 years
$25,000	277.56	210.97	179.11	161.08	149.90
30,000	333.07	253.16	214.93	193.30	179.87
35,000	388.58	295.36	250.75	225.51	209.86
40,000	444.09	337.55	286.58	257.73	239.83
45,000	499.00	379.74	322.40	289.94	269.80
50,000	555.11	421.93	358.22	322.16	299.78
60,000	666.13	506.32	429.86	386.59	359.74
70,000	777.15	590.70	501.51	451.02	419.69
80,000	888.17	675.09	573.15	515.45	479.65
90,000	999.19	759.48	644.79	579.88	539.60
100,000	1,110.21	843.86	716.44	64 4.31	599.56

7% Annual Percentage Rate

Amount of Loan	Term of mortgage				
	10 years	15 years	20 years	25 years	30 years
25,000	290.28	224.71	193.83	176.70	166.33
30,000	348.33	269.65	232.59	212.04	199.60
35,000	406.38	314.59	271.36	247.38	232.86
40,000	464.44	359.54	310.12	282.72	266.13
45,000	522.49	505.48	348.89	318.06	299.39
50,000	580.55	449.42	387.65	353.39	332.66
60,000	696.66	539.30	465.18	424.07	399.19
70,000	812.76	629.18	542.71	494.75	465.72
80,000	928.87	719.07	620.24	565.43	532.25
90,000	1,044.98	808.95	697.77	636.11	598.78
100,000	1,161.09	898.83	775.30	706.78	665.31

8% Annual Percentage Rate

Amount of Loan	Term of mortgage				
	10 years	15 years	20 years	25 years	30 years
25,000	303.32	238.91	209.11	192.95	183.44
30,000	363.98	286.70	250.93	231.54	220.13
35,000	424.65	334.48	292.75	270.14	256.82
40,000	485.31	382.26	334.58	308.73	293.51
45,000	545.97	430.04	376.40	347.32	330.19
50,000	606.64	477.83	418.22	385.91	266.88
60,000	727.97	573.39	501.86	463.09	440.26
70,000	949.29	668.96	585.51	540.27	513.64
80,000	970.62	764.52	669.15	617.45	587.01
90,000	1091.95	860.09	752.80	694.63	660.39
100,000	1213.28	955.65	836.44	771.82	733.76

9% Annual Percentage Rate

Amount of Loan	10 years	15 years	Term of mortgage 20 years	25 years	30 years
25,000	316.69	253.57	224.93	209.80	201.16
30,000	389.03	304.28	268.92	251.76	241.39
35,000	443.36	354.99	314.90	293.72	281.62
4,000	506.70	405.71	359.89	335.68	321.85
45,000	570.04	456.42	404.88	377.64	362.08
50,000	633.38	507.13	449.86	419.60	402.31
60,000	760.05	608.56	539.84	503.52	482.77
70,000	886.73	709.99	629.81	587.44	563.24
80,000	1,013.41	811.41	719.78	671.36	643.70
90,000	1,140.08	912.84	803.75	755.28	724.16
100,000	1,266.76	1,014.27	899.73	839.20	804.62

10% Annual Percentage Rate

Amount of Loan	10 years	15 years	Term of mortgage 20 years	25 years	30 years
25,000	330.38	268.65	241.26	227.18	219.39
30,000	396.45	322.38	289.51	272.61	263.27
35,000	462.53	376.11	337.76	318.05	307.15
40,000	528.60	429.84	386.01	363.48	351.03
45,000	594.68	473.57	434.26	408.92	394.91
50,000	660.75	537.30	482.51	454.35	438.79
60,000	792.90	644.76	579.01	545.22	526.54
70,000	925.06	752.22	675.52	636.09	614.30
80,000	1,057.20	859.68	772.02	726.06	702.06
90,000	1,189.36	967.14	868.52	817.83	789.81
100,000	1,321.51	1,074.61	965. 02	908.02	877.57

11% Annual Percentage Rate

Amount of Loan	10 years	15 years	Term of mortgage 20 years	25 years	30 years
25,000	344.38	284.15	258.05	245.03	238.08
30,000	413.25	340.98	309.66	294.03	285.70
35,000	482.13	397.81	361.27	343.04	333.31
40,000	551.00	454.64	412.88	394.05	380.93
45,000	619.88	511.47	464.48	441.05	428.55
50,000	688.75	568.30	516.09	490.06	476.16
60,000	826.50	681.96	619.31	588.07	571.39
70,000	964.25	795.62	722.53	686.08	666.63
80,000	1,102.00	909.28	825.75	784.09	761.86
90,000	1,239.75	1,022.94	928.97	882.19	857.09
100,000	1,377.50	1,136.60	1,032.19	980.11	852.32

Speeding up Your Loan Application Process

The Federal National Mortgage Association, otherwise known as Fannie Mae says these are some things a lender will look for as documentation from you:

Where is your down payment coming from?

It may be savings, sale of property, or life insurance properties. It can also be from relatives depending on the loan program and if it doesn't have to be repaid.

Current debts

Names and addresses of current creditors, monthly payments and balances. Bank statements may be required.

Current assets

Account numbers and balances and names of financial institutions for checking, savings, and investment accounts. Real estate and personal property can be listed on your application.

Sources of income

Two recent pay stubs and your W-2 forms for the previous two years are good verification. You must verify income from social security, pensions, dividends or interest, and rental income.

Employment information

◻ Name, address and phone number of all employers for the past seven years.

◻ Your addresses for the last seven years.

◻ Purchase agreement/sales contract. How Much Can You Borrow?

The following chart shows how much income you need to get a mortgage. Many lenders now have more lenient guidelines and may require less income, but you will pay with higher interest rates. The chart from Fannie Mae is based on a 30-year loan with 20% down payment. It assumes property taxes equal to 1.5 percent of the purchase price and hazard insurance of 0.25 percent of purchase price.

Interest Rate	Loan Amount			
	$50,000	$75,000	$100,000	$150,000
6%	$16,754	$25,131	$33,508	$50,261
6.5%	$17,451	$26,176	$34,901	$52,352
7%	$18,163	$27,244	$36,325	$54,488
7.5%	$18,889	$28,334	$37,779	$56,668
8%	$19,630	$29,445	$39,260	$58,889

8.5%	$20,383	$30,574	$40,766	$62,149
9%	$21,148	$31,722	$42,296	$63,444
9.5%	$21,925	$32,887	$43,849	$65,774
10%	$22,711	$34,067	$45,423	$68,134
10.5%	$23,508	$35,262	$47,016	$70,523
11%	$24,313	$36,470	$48,626	$72,940
11.5%	$25,127	$37,690	$50,254	$75,380

Financing and Loan Structure

A land-home package can close a couple of different ways. It is important that you know which way your loan is structured. Have your mortgage banker, broker, or loan officer give you the details.

The first way a loan can be structured	The loan closes after the home is installed and all improvements are done. Final appraisal is done, and the loan closes at the title company. Everyone is funded (land owner, dealer, contractors).
The second way a loan can be structured	There is a closing on the land to pay the seller; the improvements are done, the house is installed, final inspection; then there is a second closing and remaining money is funded to the contractors and dealer.
The third way a loan can be structured	The loan is set for four or five draws. The dealer and certain contractors are paid upon completion of their particular specialty.

Check with your contractors to let them know the kind of loan you have.

Insurance

In addition to regular Home Owner's Insurance, another type of insurance may be required on your mortgage: PMI, or Private Mortgage

Insurance. Private Mortgage Insurance is insurance that is required so that if you should die and there is nobody to pay back the loan, then an insurance company pays the loan for you. The bank, credit union, or savings and loan will require you to pay monthly insurance if you put less than 20% down toward your project. PMI can add as much as $65.00 to your monthly payment.

If you borrow $100,000.00 and put $20,000.00 down, you can avoid PMI. However, many of us don't have that much to put down, so we end up paying. Be sure to check on your equity from whomever services your loan. Once you have reached 20% equity, a lender won't necessarily tell you and gladly keep collecting PMI.

You may find, if you explore dealer financing, that their lenders don't normally require PMI. Why? Because the interest rate is so high, it causes monthly payments to be high, it can therefore put the customer out of qualifying for a loan. Additionally, the high rate of interest makes a ton of money for the lender, so it's worth the risk for them to not require insurance.

Obviously you need some kinds of insurance. But from whom and how much? From the dealership? Of course not. Insurance is required by all lenders and the friendly dealership would probably be more than happy to sell you everything you need and more, but if you buy it from them, you'll probably pay much more than you should.

First, you need homeowners insurance: flood, fire, physical damage, etc. Second, think abut looking into credit life insurance and credit disability insurance. You might need home insurance to pay off your loan should you pass away or if you were to become injured. Your payments would be made, as well. Some dealerships conveniently add these premiums to your loan, which increases your loan amount and you pay more interest.

Seek out an insurance agent for your homeowner's insurance and get two or three quotes. These will be your best bets. Your bank or credit union will have some of the best rates on credit life and disability. Think hard about credit insurance. If you're in good health and under 50, you probably won't find it a good buy. Remember, you don't have to take the insurance from the bank you're getting your loan from. Feel free to shop around.

Homeowner's Insurance: How Much Do You Need?

You need to insure the cost to rebuild the home, then add on extras, such as the cost of your central air conditioning, your furnishings and appliances, etc. There are three types of homeowner's policies: cash value, guaranteed replacement cost, and replacement cost.

Cash value is the cheapest. It pays you whatever your house and valuables would sell for today, which will probably not get you the same item. *Guaranteed replacement cost* insurance offers the best coverage, but it generally will not cover the cost of upgrading your house to meet building codes that have changed since the policy was initially put into force. *Replacement cost* insurance will replace items that were lost, but not always with the exact same item.

Homeowner's insurance also includes liability coverage up to $300,000.00. If your assets are over $300,000.00, buy more coverage.

Appreciation and Resale Value

Many people are concerned with the appreciation of a manufactured home and its resale value. Here is what I have found to be the case.

When you purchase a manufactured home, it received a title and registration because it is initially recognized as a vehicle by the state. If you place your manufactured home in a park—or on private property for that matter—and it is installed above ground, resting either on blocks or jack stands, it will be regarded as personal property, much like a car. Generally, there will be no appreciation of value to the home.

However, placed on a poured concrete foundation or basement on private property, you can convert it to real estate. It becomes appurtenant to the land; in other words, the home becomes part of the real estate. When you go to the closing at the title company, you will sign a form called "Elimination of Title." This form does exactly what its name implies: it gets rid of the title to the home and converts it to real property. The real estate then should appreciate in value.

Finding a
Good Dealer

IN MANY parts of the U.S., you can't swing a cat without hitting a manufactured home dealer. You may find 10 or 20 on the same road within 10 miles from each other. How do you find a reputable one? Take the word of a salesman on the lot? Hardly. During your shopping phase, you will eventually come across the wave of the '90s, the environmental display mega-dealer. These are the ones that have their display homes set up, furnished, and even have the lights on. Their lots look like subdivisions. A few may even have air conditioning. Very impressive, right? Maybe.

You may come across the Ma and Pa dealer with five or six homes on display. The weeds are taller than you and the office is an old single-wide. Looks like times are hard and these people really need to sell a home, right?

Yet another type of dealer you may encounter is the factory direct lot. Well, now we're talking. No middleman. Homes for Less. Really? Let's look at each one of these very carefully.

The Best Time to Buy

Usually salespeople and sales managers are pushing for a monthly and yearly quota of sales. Sales people get "spiffed" if they reach a set goal of write-ups per month.

I suggest the end of any month or anytime in December to buy. A dealer may be less apt to pull the sales game with you and just want the deal you are offering.

One more big reason to buy at these times is that the owner of the dealership gets the coveted holdback check from the manufacturer at the end of the year. Many times this money is his or her yearly pay. It can range from hundreds to thousands of dollars per home. Here's an example:

Homes sold in one year:	100
Average invoice cost per home:	$35,000
Holdback percent per invoice:	9%
Total check due dealer from manufacturer:	$315,000

That's not a bad paycheck for the year, is it? The bigger dealers that sell more of a particular brand can negotiate the holdback with the manufacturer. It can be anywhere from 2-14% per invoice (home). Note: The so-called factory-direct dealerships can have hold-back built into the home's cost as well.

Types of Manufactured Home Dealers

In the sections that follow, we'll take a look at the different types of manufactured home dealerships and compare what they can offer you.

Environmental Display, Mega-Dealers

Call them huge dealerships with huge overheads. Dealers don't normally own their display homes (or stock homes, ready for immediate delivery). They pay interest on them to flooring companies. This interest is high, normally prime plus 2 or 3 percent. Auto dealers are set up the same way. A safe figure for a dealer with 20 display homes and 10 stock homes would be $8,000 to $10,000 in interest per month. How would you like to pay that much interest every month? Then there's the power bill to pay, along with landscaping, commissions, and plenty of other overhead.

Don't fall for this environmental display ploy. This place is the equivalent of test driving a car. The whole concept is to get you in a furnished home and romance you into justifying the high price they are asking. Unfortunately, lots of emotional home buyers fall for it. Buyer beware.

Think about walking into a home with no furniture. It's cold and the carpet isn't even down. Looks barren, doesn't it? It makes a fair impression at best, with not much value here to justify the price. However, if you walked into the same place set up as a display home, furnished, with all the lights on, a bit of potpourri in the air, and the table set, wouldn't you feel more value in that home?

Don't get caught up in it. The home set-up is still the same home as the unfurnished one. Turn your buying process practical, not emotional.

More and more dealers are using this emotional buying experience, and it is working. Buying is an emotional decision for most people, and dealers know it. They capitalize on it and will take all you have.

Ma and Pa Dealerships

Now, let's turn to the small hole-in-the-wall dealer. Their lot is unkempt, the houses are pinch-parked, no carpet is laid, the doors haven't been squared and don't even shut. Here's a place to get a deal, you may think Let's see: The dealer's overhead costs may be less than they are for a larger dealer, but that is not an indicator of lower cost homes. You still need to shop around and do your own legwork.

Let's give the dealer the benefit of the doubt. He may ask a thousand or so less than his competition, but he is still getting a rebate or kickback from the factory, just like the mega-dealer. He and the in-house finance companies may be making some extra bucks from contractor referrals. Still think you're going to get a good deal?

"Factory-Direct"

Finally, what's going on with this factory direct stuff? Over the last few years, there has begun what happens with many industries: lots of mergers and buy-outs. Brand X is different than Brand Y, but yet they are both umbrellaed by the same company. Manufacturers buy a retail chain of dealerships and call them factory direct stores. These multiple brand line dealers make it impossible to tell who you are buying from. How do you know the brand you just bought in Idaho is owned by a company in North Carolina, but maintains the same Idaho name? Soon, instead of 25 different manufacturing companies, there will be 20, then 15, then 10, and so on.

It's like the big three auto makers. Over time, only the largest and strongest survived but the buyers aren't getting a better deal as a result. I believe this will continue to happen for some time to come with manufactured housing.

In my opinion, factory-direct does not really exist. Here's why. A manufacturer can't sell homes. Only a retailer can. That's why when you call the factory and ask to buy a home from them, they refer you to a retailer. It is against the law for them to sell retail. They don't have a license to sell.

When one corporation owns the factory and the retailer, it must maintain different entities. The dealership does in fact buy the home from the factory and retails it to you at the most profit it can get. The price a factory-owned retailer pays the company-owned factories is not much different from the price an independent small dealer would pay. The factory-owned store has to keep books and buy homes from the factory just like any independent dealer. It is separate from the factory. I have found that dealerships that are owned by the corporation that owns the factory will ask the most money from you. Enter at your own risk. So much for factory-direct savings.

So where are the good dealers with the good service? They are out there, but it can be tricky to find them. If you ask a dealer for references, guess what? He will give you only the good ones. That isn't going to help you. Call the state Consumer Affairs Office, the Better Business Bureau, and any other office your particular state has. Most importantly, ask your neighbors who just bought a manufactured home what their experiences was with the dealer. Remember, a pretty dealership that looks like a subdivision does not guarantee good service.

This may sound silly, but use your instincts. Instincts are generally right and can tip you off to crooks. Don't be afraid to trust your intuition.

Truth in Advertising?

In general, most printed and televised advertising that manufactured home dealers use is to pique your interest and get you to call or come if you are in the market for a home.

However, there are certain companies (especially those that own several dealerships, but smaller operations as well) that use very deceptive advertising to lure susceptible buyers into finance and home nightmares. Let's look into a few:

◻ "Divorce forces sale of home, will sacrifice huge equity."

Now you don't really believe someone would actually advertise his or her divorce in the classifieds, do you?

◻ "Missing… my wife. Please buy my new home before my aim gets better."

Yes, this ridiculous and offensive ad has been used.

◻ "Bob and Mary bought, Bob left and Mary lost. Assume $356.00 per month loan."

In this ad, there is no Bob or Mary. It's a dealer ad placed by a bored sales manager.

◻ "Abandoned home or moving, take over payments."

Two things are wrong here. First, if a home is abandoned, the bank would take the house back, and second, if someone is moving out of their home, a bank would not let them bring in a second party to "take over payments."

One more cruel hoax for you to be wary of: A retailer advertises a 1,800 sq. ft. 4-bed, 2-bath double-wide for only $39,900. I'd be amazed if you could find a quality-built, correctly optioned home for such a low price. So how can a dealer advertise that price? By not including the cost of delivery and set-up. That's another $10,000, that you won't find out about until you're in the dealer's office, pen in hand, ready to sign off on the deal. Beware.

There are other deceptive ads, but you can get a taste of the deceptive advertising from just these few examples. You may be wondering if dealers really have sales and advertise honestly. Yes, sometimes. If you negotiate up from the dealer cost of the home, I'd consider that a sale.

If you are going to fall for ads like "one dollar over invoice," or "Special Purchase," or "Factory Sale," or "Big Discount on Sale Models," or "Close-Out Sale," then I suppose you'll get taken at a "sale," like hundreds of other home buyers do. But you don't have to. Forget the ads and gimmicks. Forget low down payment plans and sales and "factory direct" pricing. Focus on the steps I will show you to get the lowest price on a new home and the maximum dollar on your trade.

Modern Sales Systems

Like so many people who have bought just about anything from anyone, I, too, have been romanced, confused, and charged just too dang much for goods and services.

I think King Solomon said it best: "There is nothing new under the sun." It's just packaged differently. Nothing could be truer when it comes to sales, salespeople, and dealership owners. Pushy, dishonest, promise-all salespeople and sales techniques are made, not born.

I have harsh words for salespeople and, at the same time, much sympathy. There are many folks who sell for a living that are well-intentioned, care-a-lot people. The problem starts during the Saturday morning sales meeting. General managers and sales managers (sales managers are the whipping boys of the general managers, and general managers get it from the owners) get pressure from their bosses to motivate, intimidate, and plain old threaten salespeople to sell. It does not matter the pecking order of the salespeople. The top dog is put under more pressure than the rookie. Why do you think the salesman of the year gets to be top dog? He or she makes the most profit for the dealership.

Quotas are set monthly and yearly for manufactured home salesmen. Write-up goals are set and salesmen often get "spiffed" for reaching the quota. How would you like to be a write-up?

Sadly, in the sales world, change comes slowly, if at all. How refreshing it would be for a salesman to actually ask you what you are looking for in a home, show you what you want, and then help you to achieve ownership in an honest way, not trying to control your every move and thought.

Think how glorious it would be if a salesman or a dealer would follow a simple set of rules: treat customers with respect and dignity; deliver everything agreed upon. This isn't rocket science. Giving people everything that was ordered isn't supposed to be that hard. Instead, so many companies, and not just manufactured home dealers, make selling a complicated technique-oriented process in which you, the "up" are an ignorant number. Confusion and control are what are in store for you unless you are prepared and take charge for yourself.

This is the single largest purchase you will ever make, or at least one of the largest. You need to know the details; don't be led around by the nose.

6.

Shopping for a Home

LET'S LOOK at a typical experience of a couple shopping for a new home. Travis and Tara are typical Americans. Travis owns his own business and Tara works as an assistant manager at a department store. They both deal with the public on their jobs and spend a good deal of time problem-solving for their customers, helping them get what they pay for.

After years of renting, they reached a decision to invest in a home and stop throwing money away as rent. The interest on their mortgage will be tax-deductible, and a home will allow a place for their kids to grow up. Travis's interest in manufactured homes was piqued when his neighbor put one on his property and it took only three days. Both Travis and Tara were impressed with the way these trailers had improved, not only in appearance but also in the materials that were used and in the construction. Additionally, the price was considerably less than building a home on site.

That Saturday is shopping day. At their first stop, they are greeted by a salesman wearing shorts, reeking of cigarette smoke. "Hi, how can we help you?" he asks.

"Well," says Travis, "we need a home."

The salesman responds, "They are all unlocked. Help yourself. I'll be in the office if you have any questions."

Travis and Tara begin walking from house to house, wandering, really, unsure of what they are seeing. Once they have seen all the homes, Tara likes several of them and needs to get some prices.

The salesman in the office quickly gives them some floor plans with some figures on them and tells them to have a nice day. Bewildered and somewhat turned around from all they had seen, they decide it's time to see another dealer.

This time, the salesman seems a bit more helpful. He seems to have some energy and has some useful information. "What is it you folks are looking for today?" he asks.

"We are in the market for a new house," Tara replies.

"Great! How many bedrooms do you need?" the salesman drools. "I've got this super house over here that's on sale and it's three bedrooms!"

Travis and Tara agree to see it, so off they go. "This home is a great buy and has many options," the salesman continues.

"What kind of options?" Travis asks.

"Well, I think the carpet is an upgrade, and this house has an optional ceiling fan."

Travis thinks the house is a bit plain and possibly too small. Tara agrees.

The salesman shoots a look in her direction and quickly suggests that for $33,900.00, they would be hard-pressed to find a home built with this quality and this many extras.

"What makes your home better than all the others?" Travis asks.

"Everyone knows this brand is the Cadillac of manufactured homes and our service is rated Number 1," responds the salesman.

"I see," Travis says quietly.

"Why don't we go in and write this one up. We have great financing here. On the spot approval," the salesman says as he begins to walk toward the office.

Tara's face begins to crinkle, because she's feeling pressured. "Let's get out of here," she whispers to Travis.

"You got it," he says, and they leave.

Frustrated and very disappointed that no one seems sincere or willing to spend time with them trying to find out what their needs are, they take a break.

"I don't get it," Tara says with a sigh. "This is turning out to be just like looking for a car."

"Yeah," Travis says. "We're talking about investing lots of money here. Why don't these places want to help us?"

Tired and suspicious, the two future homeowners decide to try one more dealership. This one has a 25-foot billboard along the expressway that reads, "Save thousands with factory-direct housing." The landscaping is immaculate and there is an inviting sign on what appears to be the office; "Information and Welcome Center" it reads.

As Travis and Tara drive up to the Welcome Center, the salesman actually comes out and greets them at their car.

Now, this is more like it, Travis thinks. What service. The salesman is wearing a tie with slacks, and doesn't have a cigarette hanging out of his mouth.

"Welcome to Humongous Homes!" he says warmly." Is this your first visit?"

"Yes," Tara says.

"Well, wonderful! Come on in to our welcome center, so I can get some information from you." the salesman says, as he turns and almost runs back to the office.

Travis thinks this is certainly the place to buy. What enthusiasm.

Travis and Tara walk into the office, following the salesman back into his cubicle. It seems very inviting and warm. There isn't a desk, but rather a small round table with four chairs around it. There isn't even a door.

"May I offer you some coffee or soda?" the salesman asks. "By the way, my name is Dave," he says, extending his hand first to Travis and then to Tara.

"I'd like a diet soda," Tara says.

"I'll take one too, regular, though," Travis says. "I'm Travis, and this is my wife, Tara."

Handing them the cold soda cans, Dave says warmly, "So this is your first visit to Humongous Homes?"

"Yep," Travis responds.

"Well, you're in for a treat. We're different from most of your manufactured home dealers. Since we are owned by the factory, we can offer huge savings and great service. Why, we even own our own bank and insurance company. Let me show you."

Dave then pulls out from under his side of the table something that looks like a colorful flip chart that he calls *The Humongous Homes Story Book*.

Comfortable in their chairs, and sipping their sodas, Travis and Tara listen intently.

Dave goes on to explain each page of the storybook by reading script written on the back of the sheet. Twenty minutes and thirty pages later, Travis and Tara are thoroughly impressed. This company is on the ball. The salesman has taken the time to tell them the history of Humongous Homes and all the services that the company offers, not to mention how well built the homes are. It's like one-stop shopping. Finance, insurance, the home. Humongous Homes would even be the general contractor for Travis and Tara.

Next, Dave asks, "In order for me to be of service to you, I need to ask you some income questions, so we know how much home you can afford. This way, I won't show you homes that are out of your reach. Besides, if you see too many homes, they just start to blend together anyway."

Travis and Tara agree.

"Tara," Dave asks," how much do you make a month?"

"About $1,200.00," Tara responds.

"Travis," Dave goes on, "how about you?"

"I bring in around $2,300. I'm self-employed, so it varies."

"Okay," Dave replies. "Let's do some figuring here and see what you can afford for a payment." He begins to punch these numbers into his calculator:

1200 + 2300 = 3,500

3,500 x 0.40 = $1,400.

(Note that Dave took 40% of $3,500 as the basis for his calculations instead of 36%. This got Travis and Tara into a higher payment.)

"Now, what are your monthly bills, not counting rent and utilities," Dave asks.

"Our car payment is $270, and we have three credit cards, on which we pay $260 a month," Tara replies.

"Great", says Dave and continues punching in numbers.

"$1,400 –$270–$260 = $870 for monthly home payments. You folks have a good income, and according to my calculations can spend just about as much as you want." Dave continues, "Have you found any property yet?"

Travis replies," No, not yet."

Dave says, "I can help you with that. We work exclusively with a realtor who can help you find land."

Tara says, "You make it sound easy." She smiles as she realizes their home buying experience is becoming much more relaxing.

At this point, Dave knows he has some good buyers and wants to continue to feed them.

"Travis and Tara, you are so much fun to work with. I can't tell you how refreshing it is to talk with people that know what they want."

Travis's chest puffs a little.

"By the way," Dave smiles, "for this month's promotion, we are giving away a free 19-inch TV to go in your new living room!" His smile becomes more enthusiastic.

"Let's look at some other figures, so we can determine how much your land and improvements might cost." Out comes the calculator.

Tara expresses a concern: "What will our total payment be? How much are these homes? How much of a loan do we qualify for?"

"Let's finish our numbers and we will know. Of course, these are just estimates for now. Let's see," Dave mumbles. "Say you find land you like for $25,000.00. Then you need a foundation. That will cost about $5,000.00. You may need a well and septic tank. That's probably $8–12,000.00. You may want a garage and a driveway. You're looking at $18,000 for that. Here's the figure I've come up with:

Land.	$25,000
Foundation	$ 5,000
Well and Septic tank	$12,000
Garage and driveway	$18,000
Total.	**$60,000**

"Wait. I'm confused, says Travis. We haven't even looked at a home yet."

Dave's reply is smooth and sounds sincere."I'm working backwards. That is, now that we know the estimated cost of your land and improvements, I can tell how much you have left for the home of your choice."

Here are the figures Dave uses to figure how much Travis and Tara can finance:

$870 monthly payments

30 year term

9.75 % interest rate

Amount they could finance: $101,262.00

"Well," Dave explains, "$101,262.00, minus $60,000 for improvements, leaves you $41,262.00 for a house; so let's go look at two or three in that price range."

"Great," says Travis. "Let's do it."

Dave doesn't even have to talk about a payment. This is perfect.

The first home Dave shows Travis and Tara is 1,100 square feet with two bedrooms and two baths. "This is a neat cottage-style home and has a great little breakfast nook," Dave says proudly.

"What's the price on this one?" asks Travis.

I believe the range is $34–36,000, depending on the options," Dave smiles.

Tara says, "I would really like three bedrooms. And I'd like a little bigger kitchen. Can we see something bigger?"

"Sure," Dave says, ushering them to a small 3-bedroom model that is 1,228 square feet.

"This is better, but we still need a bigger kitchen," Tara says.

"Let's look at one more I think is the perfect home for you," Dave says, skipping out the front door.

The third house is also a 3-bedroom home, about 1,300 square feet. "This is you!" Dave says as he opens the door. "It's right within your budget, too. $40,200.00!"

Both Travis and Tara agree that the size is adequate and the price is right for what Dave has told them they can afford.

"This feels real cozy," Tara says.

"What do you think, Travis?" Dave asks.

"I think it will work", says Travis.

"Great! Let's go and start the paperwork and get you into financing." Dave says eagerly, as he leads them back to the Welcome Center and pulls out his purchase order book. Tara finally gets the nerve to ask again, "What will our monthly payment be?"

"It will be around $850.00 per month," Dave says.

"That's a big payment," Tara says.

"Don't worry," Dave says sympathetically. "With your income, you can afford it."

Contracts and Finance Twists and Turns

Now Travis and Tara are seeing themselves in their new home. Dave has romanced them and seemed sincere. He even showed them a home in their price range that they liked. He seemed to know about finance, too. They think they have a good deal.

Dave begins to write all the required information on the purchase order: names, address, phone number, model of home, and stock number.

"Folks," he begins, "this is a lot model, so I won't need as much deposit to hold your home until financing is done, but I'm required to get at least 20% down."

"Twenty percent," Travis quips. "I don't have that much with me."

Dave replies, "You know, you are so well qualified, I'm going to talk to my sales manager to see if he would take less. I'll be right back."

"At least he's on our side," Tara says. A few moments later Buck comes in with Dave. Buck is an easy-to-talk-to guy and seems to know everyone in the area. Dave lets Buck sit in his chair.

"Hi, I'm Buck. Sounds like Dave here has helped you find the perfect home."

"Yes, he has," says Travis. "We just don't have the 20% down today."

"Tell you what," Buck says. "I'll go ahead and waive the 20% down and reduce it to 10% down. Sound okay?"

"Ten percent would be $4,090.00," Dave states, tapping his calculator again.

"Okay, says Travis. "We can do that."

"Great. Let's get the paperwork done for you," grins Buck.

Dave continues to write on the purchase order: lot model or one like it.

"What does that mean?" asks Travis.

"Travis, quite honestly, it's for Humongous Homes' protection," Dave answers. "It takes 60 to 90 days to complete a land-home package like yours, and I'm not allowed to tie up a display model for that long. This allows us to sell the home and order you another just like it. Don't worry. The price won't change."

"Well, all right. Does it really take that long?"

"Sometimes. But we try to do land-home packages in 30 days," Dave says reassuringly, holding back a chuckle.

"What do you think our interest rate will be?" Tara inquires.

Dave's answer sounds reasonable. "It depends on your credit background. "Since Travis is self-employed, it will probably be a bit higher than usual. I'm sure it will be under 10 percent, though."

Travis doesn't realize that being self-employed does not disqualify someone from getting a competitive interest rate.

Travis, concerned about his $4,000, says, "Can I get this back if we change our minds?"

"Oh, sure," Dave says. "Deposits are refundable if your credit is denied."

"That's what I was after," Travis says, relieved. "What's this $350.00 doc fee?"

Dave replies, "Our documentation fee is what you pay to cover the cost of getting you financed and all that other paperwork."

"Seems a bit high," Travis remarks.

"It's really not. Frankly, our costs are higher than you think."

Tara, curious about some of the print below where they were supposed to sign, asks Dave, "What does it mean here, where it says 'tires and axles are returned to the dealer for recycling'?"

Dave smoothly replies, "We recycle tires and axles to save you, the customer, money. Neat, huh?"

"It makes sense," Tara agrees.

Both Travis and Tara are impressed. This is a real class outfit. The salesman is genuinely concerned about them and very knowledgeable. No pressure, and easy financing. This is what we are looking for, they smile to each other.

After Dave is finished with the contract, he asks Travis and Tara to sign at the bottom. They do.

Next, Dave gets out a credit application for Travis and Tara to fill out. Surprisingly, it is only one page long and takes all of ten minutes to complete.

"Okay," Dave begins. "Next, I have to get this into finance. It shouldn't take but a few days. Why don't you two go take a look at your new home one more time."

"Sounds good," Travis says, putting an arm around Tara's shoulder as they go out the door.

"This turned out to be really easy," Tara says as they open the door to their future home. "But should we have looked at and priced more homes?" There are so many brands and many other options. I mean, I really like this home, but I guess I'm just a little nervous."

"I'm feeling a little uneasy, too. I hear what you're saying," Travis responds.

"I guess we have to do this sometime," Tara replies.

"Dave enters the home and says with a big smile, Come on out in front so I can get a picture of you two standing in front of your new home." Dave takes two pictures, one for Tara and Travis, and one for himself. This will give you a reminder of how good this home fits you while we check on your financing. I'll call you in a few days.

Travis and Tara leave Humongous Homes with a picture of their new home and a promise of financing. Overall, they are very excited and glad at how things went. Their visit did cost them $4,000, and the contract was a bit complicated, but they still feel happy.

Three days later, the phone rings at their house. It is Dave, he says quietly, "I need for you and Tara to come in. We need to discuss your financing."

All right. We'll be in this afternoon.

Dave has a serious look on his face as he meets Travis and Tara at the door. "Come back to my office, he says. Travis, Tara, we got your financing through, but it wasn't easy. Your payment is $960.00 a month."

Travis jumps. "What?"

"Just kidding," Dave grins. "We got your payment for $890.00 per month."

"That's better," Tara sighs with relief." It isn't the $850 that Dave had originally said, but at least it wasn't $960 a month. Dave has a good sense of humor, she decided.

"We ended up going with our company-owned bank because Travis's self-employment status presented some real difficulties to other finance companies," Dave says, showing some concern. "What we need to do now, he continues, is get land tied up for you and start the improvements. I'll call Lola. She can show you properties tonight if you like."

"Sounds great!" Travis and Tara say together, sounding excited.

After Travis and Tara find property and make an offer, Dave begins to report to them on bids for improvements, using the costs he had originally given:

Foundation	$ 5,000
Well	$ 8,000
Septic	$ 4,000
Garage	$16,000
Driveway	$ 2,000
Total:	**$39,000**

Dave knows the cost of these improvements is less, but it increases his profit and gives him a bigger commission. He orders an appraisal of the project, as all lenders require an appraisal. Since it is a busy time of the year for appraisers, it takes almost three weeks. Once the appraisal is finished, it is time to start the improvements on the property. The well is dug, followed by the septic tank installation. The contractor doing the foundation is booked, so he can't begin for a good two weeks. Finally he finishes the foundation and starts on the garage. During this time, Dave sells the home Travis and Tara put money down on (remember "lot home or one like it?"). Humongous Homes orders another one for Travis and Tara, but the factory is four weeks out, so more time is added to the process.

The garage is completed and the house finally comes off the factory line, is delivered and set on the foundation. Ten days later, the house is done and Travis and Tara can finally close the deal.

As the credit manager is going over their loan papers, Travis notices the amount to finance was higher than he had thought.

He asks, "What happened to this figure? $101,262 package cost less $4,090 down payment equals $97,172 amount to finance."

"Well," the loan officer begins, "we are adding your closing costs to your amount to finance. The closing costs are $2,200.00. Your monthly payment is $920.00."

"What?" Tara gasps. "We were told that it would be $890.00." She and Travis look at each other with consternation.

"We can do it," Travis says reassuringly. "Our house is delivered. The improvements are done. We can move in. It's okay. It'll be tough, but we can do it."

Travis signs first, and Tara signs with visible reluctance, and returns an uncertain smile to Dave's congratulations to the new home owners.

Analysis of the Story

This is a somewhat abbreviated story, but it demonstrates the experience many purchasers of manufactured homes go through. Let's see what Travis and Tara did wrong.

The biggest, most costly mistake was not doing any preparatory homework. It cost them time and money, and will stretch their income thin each and every month. I'm not saying they are stupid. They just trusted the wrong people—the salesman and the dealer.

First, before they even looked at any homes, they should have gone to a bank, a credit union, or a mortgage broker and gotten pre-qualified. Then they needed to apply for a loan and wait for approval, so they would know the exact amount they could borrow, the down payment, the closing costs, the interest rate, and the terms of the loan.

Next, they a should have sat down and determined what payment they were comfortable with, including taxes and insurance. Many lenders require that homeowners pay monthly on their taxes and insurance. Travis and Tara's payment ended up at $920.00. If you include a monthly tax and insurance payment, their total would be around $1060.00 a month.

Remember, even if you have less than perfect credit, don't go to the dealer for financing. Call a mortgage broker. You will get a better rate and not put so much profit in a dealer's pocket.

Because Travis and Tara did not have a clear idea of the size of home they needed, and failed to look at several, they settled for a home that they were unsure of. They took the word of a salesman who took over their home buying process.

The contract was another stumbling block for Travis and Tara. Dave wrote "Lot model or one like it." This gave the dealer the right to sell the house to another buyer who could take delivery sooner. Obviously, you can tell from their story, that Travis and Tara's home was indeed sold to someone else, and it cost them several more weeks of waiting. It's a good thing their landlord was easy to get along with.

Thirty days is not realistic for a home-land package. Ninety days is much more like it, and it sometimes takes longer. Dave was a bit optimistic.

Travis was smart to ask if he could get his deposit back. Humongous Homes was smarter (slicker) by having the contract preprinted with "Deposit is fully refundable if credit is denied." What you have to realize is if a dealer gets financing approved at a lender for you and you decide you don't like the terms, you lose your deposit. Don't sign that.

The next thing questioned was the doc fee. $350.00 for what? I believe this charge was swiped from the car dealers. A documentation fee will consist of the cost to apply for title to your home. It varies, depending on what state you live in. I can't imagine that it would ever be more than $50.00. The dealer was cutting himself in for lots of profit here, too.

Next, Tara wondered what the tire and axle recycle clause meant. It's simple, really. You pay for the tires, axles, and the dealer takes them back and sells them. Isn't that a deal!

After Travis and Tara filled out the credit application, Dave invited them out to see their home again and to get a picture. What better way to remind Travis and Tara of that house? This technique is a real lock-in for customers while they're waiting for finance approval. By taking two pictures, if Travis and Tara backed out of the deal, Dave still has a picture to hang on his wall for prospective customers to see.

The approval came back and Dave used a bit of shock therapy to soothe Travis and Tara into a higher payment. Read that part again. The payment went from $850 to $960, and back to $890. What was going on?

Check carefully how long it took to do an appraisal and improvements. This part is not unusual, so be ready. The part that really hurt is when the dealer took advantage of the contract that Travis and Tara signed allowing the home to be sold to someone else. That took another month for delivery of the replacement home.

Also, Travis and Tara should have talked to their neighbor about his experience with his manufactured home.

Finally, since Dave's knowledge of finance was minimal, he didn't mention closing costs and that they would be added to the total amount to finance, thus increasing the payment. Travis and Tara were so far along in the process, they felt obligated to sign off on the loan, but if you go back to our worksheet on finance, you'll see that their payment was more than their financial situation would allow.

As you can see, Dave was trained very well, probably by his company's "Sales Trainer." This is the guy who exclusively trains all new salespeople and indoctrinates them into a particular style of selling. In the case described above, the salesperson was taught just enough to be smooth and sound knowledgeable. His company showed him how to give only a limited amount of information to customers, and to participate in a lot of partial truths and "turnovers" (see Glossary on pages 154).

Look for these telltale signs when you enter a dealership:

◻ All homes locked with signs on them that read something like, "To protect this home for its future owner, all homes are kept locked."

◻ The salesperson won't show you a home until you sit down in the office to get the pitch, that is, a flip-chart story book

◘ The salesperson tries to qualify you, get your name, and asks if you have been elsewhere.

◘ The salesperson wants you to finance and insure with the dealership.

◘ A salesperson meets you at your care, welcomes you, then asks you to come into the office and doesn't wait for a reply and walks off.

Travis and Tara just endured and fell for a completely scripted situation. Sadly, this is all Dave was trained to do, and yes, as you can see, it usually works. He practices what his sales trainer has taught him: "You must make 28 demonstrations to get 7 write-ups."

Demonstrations? What is this, a car? These companies work on large numbers and quotas. Many pay their salespeople a monthly draw; it could be $1,200. When a salesperson sells a home, the commission is applied toward the accumulated draw. If it takes three months to close a land-home package and the salesperson has racked up a $3,600 draw, but his commission is only $1,300, then he or she is "in the hole" by $2,300. It's no wonder the annual turnover for salespeople is 80 to 90 percent. Humongous homes, being as big as they are, will go through hundreds of salespeople a year. Smaller dealers can have similar training programs as well. There are a lot of consulting firms that do sales training in a less than reputable way. You deserve better.

Price

Unlike automobile companies, manufactured home companies are not required to put a Manufacturer's Suggested Retail Price (MSRP) in a window. The only way to find the exact cost a dealer paid for the home is to have exact costs for setup and delivery (and everything it entails). Plus, you would need to know the holdback the dealer gets from the manufacturer. It is highly unlikely you will be able to gather all these figures. But perhaps you can come close by using the example below and doing some homework.

Many retailers use PAC's. PAC is a term used to describe a cost of setting a home up. These prices will vary from state to state and from dealer to dealer. If you can talk the retailer into giving you a list of all the subcontractors they use to complete the set-up of your home, you can call them and get their bids.

Dealer invoice is what the dealership paid the factory for the home. Actually that's not quite true. The invoice has kickbacks, or VIP-money, built into it. These kickbacks are paid to the dealer once a year and are incentives for him to sell homes. This figure is anywhere from 2% to 11% of the price per home—and sometimes even more. Don't plan on the dealer ever giving up this money, even thought it is really your money. The invoice on a manufactured home will have the base cost to the dealer, the cost of the options, and the freight. From time to time, a rebate will appear, but you will never know. Because of this holdback money and depending on the deal the retailer negotiates with the manufacturer, different dealers can end up paying different prices for the same home.

Below is a typical cost chart for set-up of single-, double-, and triple-wide manufactured homes. The list is not exhaustive, but it covers the basics.

	Single-wide	Double-wide	Triple-wide
Freight from factory	350	675	1,500
Set-up and finish work	1,400	2,300	3,500
Carpet laying	0	300	600
House cleaning	75	150	350
Tape and texture close-up	600	1,200	1,950
Total PAC	**$2,425**	**$4,625**	**$7,900**

As you can see, it is a huge undertaking to deliver and set up a manufactured home. By the time all is said and done, there will have been six to eight subcontractors working on your home. Use this list as a base, not as exact figures. Because there's no MSRP posted on the home, I've devised this table as an approximate guide that will get you close to what the dealer paid for the home.

The following steps show you how you go about getting a handle on the dealer's price to help you establish a fair price for you.

1. Ask the dealer for his base price. If he won't give you one, walk out.

2. Ask what the base price includes (delivery and setup, freight, tape and texture, etc.). Generally the base price will include delivery to your site, but setup options will be extra.

3. Deduct from the base price the appropriate PAC. (Base that number on the figures in the chart above.)

Example:

Dealer base price: . . . . $45,000 (double-wide)

PAC 4,625

Home price $40,375

Of the $40,375 remaining, a percentage is profit, and the balance is the dealer invoice. Start high. Figure 23% of that is profit. This isn't always true. Some dealers sell at a lower profit margin and make a living on kickbacks.

Profit: $40,375 x .23 = ... $9,286.25

Dealer cost: $40,355 – $9,286.25= $31,088.75

Dealer Invoice is $31,088.75. His kickback will be between $620.00 and $3,000.00.

Shop Around

Who is going to give you the best deal? It pays to shop around. Put on your walking shoes.; it's the most valuable homework you'll ever do. If possible, visit 3 different dealers who sell the brand you're interested in. At the first stop, sit down with a salesman and spec out a house with the options and upgrades you would like. Have them give you a total delivered and set-up price. Then request a copy of the options. Tell the salesman you need to study everything at home. If they object, say that's what you do before you buy anything. If the dealership won't part with an option sheet, say good-bye and walk out.

Take the list you finally do get to two other dealers and have them give you a price on the exact same house. Tell the salesperson that you are shopping and *do not* tell him the prices you have gotten from the other dealers. Don't forget to get their base price. Also, remember to take copies for yourself, so an unscrupulous dealer doesn't do some adding and subtracting on the options sheet. Leave that original one in the car.

So, you're thinking, why can't I just call and get the dealer's base price? The answer is because you will get low-balled on the phone every time, to get you to come see them in person.

What is a fair profit for a dealer to make on a house? $5,000, $10,000, $15,000? How about $2,000 or $1,000? Here are some typical markups on single-, double-, and tripe-wide homes for you to consider during your calculations:

Single-wide	18–23 %
Double-wide	19-24%
Triple-wide	20-26%

A realistic profit for the dealer should probably end up between $3,000 and $5,000. That's better than $10,000 or more, isn't it? The profit will be less on a single-wide than on a triple-wide, with the double-wide somewhere in the middle. I have seen profit on the sale of a triple section home push $20,000. Ouch!

Your goal is to find the least amount of profit a dealership will take through

¤ Negotiation

¤ Beating the sales techniques

¤ Studying the specs on a house, comparing apples to apples.

Remember: "He who speaks first loses!"

7.

Finding a Home for Your Home

TO DECIDE whether to put your home in a mobile home park or on your own land, there are several deciding factors: your financial condition, your own personal goals, whether you want low maintenance, and your age.

Comparing Pros and Cons

Let's first look at financial condition. Here's a chart to compare:

Home on own land

Home	$50,000.00
Land	$20,000.00
Improvements	$15,000.00
Miscellaneous	$ 5,000.00
Total	**$90,000.00**

And here's how it works out in terms of monthly cost:

Total cost.	$90,000.00
Down payment (10%)	-9,000.00
Amount to finance:	$81,000.00
Principal and interest (at 7.5%, 30 years)	$566.36
Monthly taxes and insurance	120.00
Total monthly payment	**$686.36**

Home, renting space:

Home	$50,000.00
Improvements required by landlord:	$600.00 to $1,200.00
10% down on house	$5,000
Amount to finance	$45,000
Principal and interest (at 9.5%, 25 years)	$494.16
Monthly insurance	40.00
Space rent	275.00
Total monthly payment	**$708.16**

Let's look at the pros and cons of owning a home and land.

Pros:

1.   Your home won't depreciate (instead, it'll probably appreciate in value if it's on a foundation.

2.   You can do what you want on your land as far as improvements, within state and local zoning laws.

3.   You can have elbow room.

4.   You get a lower interest rate, thus, lower payments.

5. You own everything.

Cons:

1. None that I can think of.

Next, let's look at the pros and cons of placing a home in a park.

Pros:

1. In 55 and older parks, there's probably little or no yard work or outside maintenance.

2. Some of the better parks and communities are gated and have their own security.

3. You can move your home more easily.

Cons:

1. You have to do exactly as the rules and covenants say.

2. Your home may not appreciate in value.

3. If you decide to move your home, it will be costly and hard on your home.

4. The space rent can, and probably will, go up.

5. Sometimes management of parks can be very grouchy and hard to deal with.

6. Any improvements you make and spend money on usually stay there if you move.

7. Parks are becoming increasingly picky on the age of homes they allow.

If you are at an age of retirement or do not want to worry about yard work, and you are comfortable with the park's community rules, then renting in a park may be for you.

Right now, interest rates are low and lenders are very liberal with lending money, even to those with poor credit. Look at the payment for a park versus private property. These two figures tell a huge story. If you follow the steps in this book, ownership is easy and you won't regret it.

Mobile Home Parks

The following is a generic list of guidelines and rules you may encounter if you are going into a mobile home park or community. This list is, of course, not exhaustive, but will give you an idea of what is allowed and tells you restrictions parks will place on you. Read them carefully to make sure a rented space is for you. Pay special attention to rules number 27 and 28.

Number 27 allows the management or owner to approve or disapprove of a potential buyer, should you ever decide to sell your home. Do not accept this. A park owner does this to say no to all buyers that make good offers on your house. He will then make a lowball offer on your house and you have to sell to him. He then sells it for a high profit.

Number 28 is very bad, too. Make sure something is in writing that is specific about how much rent can be raised and in what time frame. The way it is phrased is too vague.

If these guidelines and rules don't correspond with how you envision your lifestyle, mobile home parks may not be the ideal place for your home.

Typical Park Guidelines

Guidelines are standards for new home installations and for improvements made by existing tenants at resale or replacements.

1. Fences:	New fences may be a maximum of 36 inches high and enclose only the rear one third of the lot. Fences may be chain link with a top rail, wood, or wood-look vinyl. Wood fences can be solid or picket type. All fences should have at least one access gate. Upon

sale and/or occupancy change of existing homes, all front yard fencing must be removed and fences higher than 36 inches should be removed or reduced to 36 inches.

2. Deck and Steps: Deck and steps must be skirted to match home skirting. Manufactured steps must be installed at all doorways. Railings are required. All wood should be painted or stained to match the color of the home. Color coordinated outdoor carpeting is encouraged. Temporary steps must be removed within 60 days of occupancy.

3. Sheds: Sheds may be wood or metal but must match the home in color. No more than two sheds are allowed. Sheds must be placed at the rear of the driveway.

4. Storage: All RV's, boats, and extra vehicles must be stored in the storage area, not at the home site. If the storage area is full, items must be stored off-site.

5. Awnings: Newly installed homes must have awnings installed within 90 days. A minimum 10 ft. x 40 ft. patio awning and all entry doors must have an awning cover. If the space has a side driveway, parallel to the home, a driveway awning will be required. Awnings may be required on existing homes at sale and/or occupancy change.

6. Antennas: Antennas or satellite dishes must be approved in writing. They may be located on the roof away from the street or at the rear of the home out of sight. Dishes must be 18 inches or smaller.

7. Landscaping: The entire lot must be landscaped within 90 days of move-in. Drought resistant landscaping is highly recommended. Landscaping must include some plants. Small gardens may be planted at the rear of home site, but should not be visible from the street.

Typical Park Rules

The following rules are for the protection and welfare of the tenants and visitors to this mobile home park. Any violation of the rules will be sufficient to commence legal eviction proceedings to have the tenant and the mobile home removed from the park. The management reserves the right to alter any of the following rules upon ninety (90) days written notice.

1.   Tenant and any occupant must register and be listed at the Park Manager's Office prior to moving the mobile home into place.

2.   The mobile home must be set in place by a company approved by the management and placed on the lot only as specified by management within thirty (30) days of executing the rental agreement.

3.   All mobile homes will be inspected by management prior to placement in the park. Management will prohibit placement of any mobile home which, in management's sole discretion, fails to meet the minimum park requirements or established National Mobile Home Standards. Tenant's mobile home shall be in good repair and must bear a current annual license or State identification number.

4.   Skirting is required to be installed within sixty (60) days after the mobile home is placed on the lot. Removable tongues and hitches shall be taken off prior to skirting. Permitted skirting materials are manufactured metal skirting that matches the home, wood if the home is wood, or masonry. Vents must be installed for safety.

5.   Each space is provided with a driveway for parking. Tenant may not alter driveway or walkways without prior approval of the manager. Any approved concrete added by the Tenant shall be done to professional standards.

6.   Each mobile home space must be identified by a space number. Space numbers of 3 inches should be affixed to each mobile home.

7.   All utility hookup connections from the existing electrical, water, sewer, telephone, and gas lines, if any, must comply with local and

state regulations, and any wiring, plumbing or other hookup costs whatsoever, are the responsibility of the tenant. Electrical connections must be made by a licenses electrician.

8. All tenants' garbage, trash or refuse shall be kept in covered metal or plastic containers which must be periodically cleaned and free from any obnoxious odor and/or insects, and must be placed in or at the rear of the tenant's mobile home in an inconspicuous place or at the place designated by management.

9. The tenant shall keep and maintain the premises in a neat, clean, and orderly condition and free of debris. The tenant shall also water, mow, and trim the tenant's lawn and care for any shrubbery and perform ice and snow removal when needed. If the tenant fails to do any of the above, the management will order the work completed to park standards and all costs of such work will be charged to the tenant, which costs will be treated as additional rent and payable by the first of the following month. Tenant will receive an itemized billing of such charges when incurred.

10. Awning, patio enclosure, any construction, or other improvements on the lot must be approved in writing by the management. Approval shall only be granted after plans or proper description have been submitted to the management. All construction and improvements shall meet all applicable state and local codes.

11. Any requests for improvements, alterations, fencing, landscaping, gardening, planting of shrubs, flowers, trees, or other exterior improvements must be submitted in writing and will be allowed only with the management's prior written approval. The tenant shall not make any penetrations into the ground, such as placing posts, stakes, etc., that might interfere with underground utilities, without the management's prior written approval. The height of any extensions that exceed four (4) feet above the tenant's mobile home must be approved in writing by the management. Any improvements, the removal of which would significantly damage the landscape of the mobile home lot, shall not be removed by the tenant when vacating the park. If the tenant removed improvements when vacating, the tenant shall leave the lot in better then or substantially the same condition as upon taking possession.

12. Vehicular traffic within the park shall not exceed ten (10) miles per hour and shall stop to give pedestrians the right-of-way. Tenants or guests of tenants are not to walk through or trespass upon other lots or use vacant lots for any purpose.

13. Vehicles not in regular use, pickups larger than 3/4 ton, boats, boat trailers, campers, trailers, snowmobiles, other recreational vehicles may not be stored in the park except in a separate storage area, if available. Inoperative vehicles and unlicenced vehicles must be stored outside of the park.

14. Off-street parking is provided at the tenant's mobile home space. Tenant shall not park any vehicles in the park's streets except for loading or unloading unless special arrangements are made with the management. Visitors' cars may be parked only in front of the tenant's space for a short period of time.

15. Wading pools, swings, slides, and other similar types of equipment shall not be permitted on lawns, unless the tenant obtains prior approval in writing by the management.

16. Space under and around the tenant's mobile home must be kept clean and sanitary at all times, and nothing shall be stored under the mobile home until the mobile home has been properly skirted and the type of storage has been approved by the management. Other outside storage is not allowed except in a storage shed approved in writing by the management as to type, color, manufacturer and location. Standard yard and patio furniture, barbecue equipment and approved lighting equipment are permitted in the tenant's space and must be kept in good condition. No fuel, oil or other materials of combustible nature shall be stored under or near the mobile home, or anywhere in the park, if it is considered a danger to others. The hanging of clothes on an outside clothesline is allowed only at the rear of the space. A small amount of cut and neatly stored fire wood may be kept at the space.

17. Trespassing, loud or disturbing noises, the use of motorcycles or motor bikes within the park, obnoxious odors, and/or other disturbances or conduct by a tenant or his guest that is offensive or violates other tenants' or management's right to quiet and

peaceful enjoyment of the park will not be tolerated and subject the tenant to eviction from the park.

18. The tenant agrees NOT to keep pets on or within the park unless otherwise approved in writing by the management. If small pets are permitted, they must measure less than 18 inches high at the shoulders, fully grown, and must be kept within the tenant's mobile home. The tenant must register such pets with the management and must show proof of immunization for any pet subject to rabies. Dogs or cats must be neutered. Any pet that becomes a problem for any tenant or management shall be removed from the park immediately by the tenant at the request of the management. Pets, other than those owned by tenants, will not be permitted on the park premises. Cages or dog houses are not permitted outside the home. Pets outside the home must be on a leash at all times. This paragraph does not imply that pets will be allowed.

19. Homes must be periodically washed and/or painted as may be necessary to maintain an attractive appearance. It shall be done in such a manner so as not to cause damage or be a nuisance to the adjoining residents.

20. Residents must provide heat tapes to protect waterlines from freezing. These tapes must be connected to the home's utilities at the time of the initial hook-up. Residents will be held responsible for the expense to repair frozen water lines on the resident's lot. The tenant shall notify the management of any water hydrant problems immediately.

21. The resident's home or lot must not be used for any business or commercial operation, including the sale of trailers, vehicles, or other type of merchandise or by providing a service to members of the public at the tenant's home. If you desire to sell your mobile home, you must first advise the management of your intent. "For sale" signs must be approved by the park management in advance and situated next to your home or in a window. Contact park management for assistance they may be able to provide you.

22. All vehicles must conform to local laws regarding emissions and repairs. Corrective action must be made immediately when

requested by the management. Vehicles dripping oil or gas must be repaired in a timely way and drip spots on parking surfaces must be cleaned by the resident. Repairs, tune-ups, oil changes or overhauling of motor vehicles are not permitted in the park.

23. A recreation building, storage area, and other facilities, if furnished, are for the tenant's enjoyment and use. The tenant must abide by the rules and regulations posted by the management at the respective facilities. All persons using the park facilities do so at their own risk.

24. Solicitors, vendors, peddlers, and other similar business activities are considered an intrusion, and are not permitted in the park. Necessary delivery men who are authorized by management may have access to the park.

25. Violations of any law or ordinance of the city, county, state, or federal government will not be tolerated and are sufficient reason for eviction. Acts will not be permitted which could place the management or owner of these premises in violation of a law or ordinance of the city, county, state, or federal governments. The tenant shall pay all taxes on his mobile home and improvements due by reason of any federal, state, county, or municipal law.

26. The management reserves the right of access to the tenant's lot at any time for the purposes of inspection or utilities maintenance and to temporarily move tenant's mobile home for repairs of any of the Park's facilities.

27. The management reserves the right to approve or disapprove of any potential buyer the tenant may wish to sell his/her mobile home to.

28. The management reserved the right to adjust rent according to the market condition.

Moving Your Manufactured Home

Even if you are a single-wide buyer, or double-wide for that matter, it is important to realize that these homes aren't your grandma's trailer anymore. Please don't think you can move these homes overnight to a different location. A 14 x 70 ft. single-wide entails much more to move than they used to—not to mention the expense. Let me give you an idea of cost here:

Tires and axles charge	$200.00
Tear down of skirting, awnings	$500.00
Freight to new site	$800.00
New set-up	$1200.00
Re-skirt	$600.00
Tape and texture repair	$200.00–$500.00
Total	**$3,500.00+**

Surprising, isn't it? If you ever have to move, plan on selling your house right where it sits, unless you have family and friends to do this work for you.

Trading Homes

Let's talk about trades. You have lived in a 1977 single-wide and now it's time to get into something a bit nicer and newer. Watch out: here's what can happen and how to protect yourself.

Many dealerships don't post the prices of their model homes. Rather, the salesperson will give you ranges of cost that depend on how the house is equipped. Don't fall for this. One of the first things a salesman will ask you is if you have a trade. That way he will know if he has to inflate the price of the new home to accommodate your trade. This is most common, but there are a few dealers that will deduct what you want for your trade from their retail price, which is inflated already.

Here is the best thing you can do if you have a trade. If you own it free and clear, you're in a better position than most. First, get a wholesale trailer trader to give an actual cash value appraisal of your home. Try to get at least two appraisals. Be ready: older homes do not have as much value as you may think. Your 1977 single-wide is probably worth wholesale about $3,500.00 if it is in good condition. $3,500.00 is what the wholesaler will pay you; then, in turn, he will turn around and sell it at retail for around $6,000.00.

This figure can vary in different part of the country, of course. Next, you can try to sell your home yourself. Advertise in the paper or nickel ads. Be prepared to dicker a little. Make whoever buys your house responsible to have it moved; you have enough to deal with already.

Of course, the most hassle-free way to sell your house is to let the wholesaler buy it. No muss, no fuss. You won't make quite as much, but it's the quickest way.

If you owe money on your home and want to trade, you need to find out whether your home is worth more than you owe. The way to determine the value of your house is to have the wholesale trailer trader give you a written bid. He will use a blue book for trailers. Your next route is to simply look in your neighborhood or town to see what comparable trailers are selling for. At this point, if you are "upside-down," you must make a decision. Stay in your home a few more years or trade your house in at a dealer's and add the balance of what you own to the new loan. Doesn't it sound like we're trading a car here? If you're smart, try to sell your home first, hopefully, for a few thousand more than you owe, if you can't stay put until the situation changes. Don't rush it, because that will cost you dearly.

A favorite ploy of many dealers is to advertise massive trade-in allowances for your trade. But when you check further, you will find that the promotion applies only to non-advertised homes. This is because you already know the price of their advertised homes and now they can't increase their price to "allow" for what you want for your trade. The dealer will make you order a home so he can adjust the selling price.

If you must trade your home in and you own it free and clear, follow the information in Chapter 6 to figure the approximate dealer cost of the new home (based on a final delivered and set-up cost with the options you want). Once a negotiated price is reached, then tell the salesperson that you have a trade.

Have the dealer look at your trade and tell you what they will give for it. If it is not what the trailer trader has quoted you, tell them you have had the house appraised at a certain price and that is what you want for it. The salesperson may turn green at this point and bring in his sales manager, but if you stick to your guns, you'll win.

Land Improvements

Owning your own property can be the most satisfying and secure feeling you can have. It does take some work, however. Consider where you live before you buy. People who live where it snows can run into city and county restrictions that prohibit manufactured homes. In many cases, the federal regulation overrides the state or local restriction. It can take a visit to the City Attorney or to a Planning and Zoning committee meeting, so be prepared.

As manufactured homes have changed, so have many zoning laws. In many places, you may place a double-wide or triple-wide as long as you install it on a poured concrete foundation, pour sidewalks, and whatever else the city or county requires. You may need an 80 lb. roof load for snow or some type of retaining wall somewhere on your property.

Foundation

People use the word a bit loosely, so let's clarify what a foundation really is. A foundation is concrete, poured from a cement truck in between form boards. The size of the footers and stem walls will vary depending on the building codes in your area and the manufacturer's specifications. There will be poured or pre-formed pads placed every so many feet under the I-beams and marriage line of the home, depending on the manufacturer's requirements. Refer to Fig. 7.1; what you see there is a typical foundation.

If you were to set a home in a park without the perimeter foundation, then they'd be supports only in the center. Some manufactured homes are placed on a basement foundation. In some cases, the owner has to have it for the building inspector before a

Fig. 7.1 Typical poured concrete foundation for a double-wide manufactured home.

building permit is issued, but again, I do not normally advise basements. They are expensive and most manufactured homes are not designed to be placed on a basement. If you need the extra room, it's better to just get a bigger home.

There seems to be confusion between the above description of a foundation and what is called a block foundation. A block foundation is built of cinder blocks. Unlike a solid, poured foundation, the perimeter of the home does not rest on the block foundation.

Manufactured homes are designed to be supported by cinder block or jack stands solely under the length of the I-beam and marriage line. The solid perimeter foundation was developed to satisfy banks to achieve real estate status and therefore qualify for financing. It also brings the level of the home down closer to the ground to give it a house look. In addition, the weight of the home is evenly distributed over the walls of the foundation and throughout the support system under the entire home.

Cinder block foundations will achieve the house look and are a bit cheaper but, personally, I would spend a little extra money and go with the poured foundation. Resale value will be better and I believe there will be less settling in the house, and consequently not as much need for texture repair in the interior, especially with large double- and triple-section homes.

Fig. 7.2. A two-car garage with roof pitch sloping to the sides, rather than front and rear, for more favorable rainwater drainage, away from the entrance.

Well and Sceptic Tank

Concerning wells, discuss this issue with a well driller. He can tell you how deep you may need to drill and how many horse power are required for pumping, depending on your needs.

The size of your septic tank depends on the number of bedrooms in the house. Talk to an expert about this and the tank location.

Garage and Other Improvements

The next big improvement is a garage. You may attach it to the house or have it free-standing. Get bids on both. It's better to have it a bit larger than you may think. Do you need extra room for a bench to tinker? How many cars do you have? Make sure the pitch of the roof matches that of the house, and if the garage isn't larger than a two car, consider building the pitch of the roof so snow and rain will slide to the sides of the garage and not to the front. Think about any other buildings you may need as well.

Landscaping, fences, driveways, gravel, how to bring electric power into the site, hooking up city sewer and water, and any other item you may need should be discussed with a specialized contractor and local building authorities.

Basements

Honestly, a basement is not a good financial proposition. My experience with basements is that they are very expensive. Expect to pay at least $40,000.00 for a 28 x 60 foot daylight basement with 9-foot walls. The other reasons I would not recommend this route are that many manufacturers won't build the stairwell hole into the floor and manufactured homes do not lend their floor plans to a stairway. There are more reasons besides cost and location of the stairway, but let me end here and suggest buying a bigger home instead.

8.

Finding the Best House

OF COURSE, I have my personal opinion on this matter, but you need to do your own research to learn which home will be the best for your money, based on what you know about what you can afford. (You've already gone to a bank or mortgage broker, right?)

The following pages have a checklist for you to follow as you visit manufactured home dealerships. It is important to sit down and think about which options and upgrades you really need and which ones you want.

There are certain options I will address that I believe to be essential, followed by some that you should consider, and finally, some options to avoid.

Do not allow the salesman to talk you into a particular option because it's a good buy "only from the factory." This is usually not true. There are certain items that you have to order from the manufacturer, but many are less expensive from your local hardware store and can be easily installed by you yourself. In general, dealerships will not mark up options from the factory and don't care which ones you want. Their money is made on a profit from the house. Here's how it works:

The manufacturer of the home doesn't offer the color of carpet you want, so you have to live with the 10 or so choices from the dealer's color board, right?

Wrong.

First, find out how many square yards of carpet are used in the house. Go to a carpet store and get a quote on the color you want and get at least 52 ounce carpet. Come back to the dealer and ask for the factory credit on the carpet. Unfortunately, the credit is not as much as the dealer paid; but it is better than nothing. With the price of a good carpet in hand, including installation, simply add it to the price of the house. Then on the contract to purchase, simply add: "Humongous Homes to pay Cal's Carpet House up to $2,000.00 (or whatever is the price of the carpet). This concept can work with many different options in your house, such as valances, mini-blinds, appliances, and light fixtures.

Recommended Factory Options

Here is a list of options that I recommend you have installed at the factory, unless you are a heck-of-a-good do-it-yourselfer:

Fig. 8.1 Right. 12-inch wide eves like these give a more residential look to the house.

Fig. 8.2 Below. An outside water hose connection is an important option to include.

1. Outside water faucets—at least two. Put one on each end of the house or put one each near the front and back doors, depending on the floor plan and how you set your house on the site.

2. Widest eaves(roof overhangs) available. Many manufacturers put 12" eaves standard on the ends and sides of their houses, but they will make you pay for this item. Buy it. Wide eaves keep the weather off your siding and give a better appearance to your home.

3. Air conditioner ready. This gives the home an extra "J" box under the house. This option is necessary if you are going to have an air conditioner installed. It also gives you a thermostat that allows you to switch from the furnace to the air conditioner.

4. Consider a meter base; if you are going to have underground power, this option puts an electric meter base on the side of your house.

5. Heavy insulation package—2 x 6 walls, 2 x 6 floors, vinyl-clad dual-pane widows, R-33 insulation in the ceiling, R-19 in the walls, and R-33 in the floor. I use this term to cover whatever the particular manufacturer offers in the way of additional insulation. It doesn't matter what part of the country you live in, you need to hold in heat or cool air.

6. Steel front door, 36 inches wide. It should be an inswing door.

7. Asphalt or fiberglass 3-tab shingles

8. Preferably vinyl siding, or at a minimum hardboard.

Kitchen

1. Solid wood cabinets. Don't try to save money on cabinets. Buy solid wood. Anything else will fall apart in a short time.

2. Plumbing for ice maker. If you have a refrigerator that has an ice maker, you need to have the plumbing built into the floor.

3. Garbage disposal. If you want a garbage disposal, have the factory install it. I have had to go in after the fact to install one and it was a huge and costly project.

4. Adjustable shelves. These generally come with solid wood cabinetry, but check first. You really need them.

5. Tile backsplashes. No wood, because it gets wet and will crack.

6. Metal single-lever faucets and metal shut-off valves under the sink. It is important to have this in the kitchen for ease of operation. Most of the time, manufacturers will install a decent brand of faucet. Remember, no plastic.

7. Two fluorescent lights.

8. Overhead lights in the pantry. Some manufacturers cut costs by not putting lights where they are really needed.

Utility room

1. Plug-in for freezer

Fig. 8.3 Left. Recessed entry with 36-inch insulated steel-clad inswing door.

Fig. 8.4 Below. Double stainless steel kitchen sink with single-lever metal faucet.

2. Cabinets above the washer and dryer area. Don't settle for just a shelf. You need as much storage as you can get.

3. Minimum 40-gallon water heater (50-gallon is preferable). Get a gas water heater, if possible, for economical operation.

4. No polybutylene plumbing. Many manufacturers use a high grade of plastic (ABS), which works fine. However CPVC is even better.

5. Rear 36-inch inswing door. You need this to move furniture and appliances in and out of your house.

All bathrooms

1. Metal faucets and metal shut-off valves under the sink. Remember, no plastic fixtures.

2. Porcelain or vitreous china washbasins. Plastic basins tend to melt when a curling iron is near. Vitreous china is becoming more

Fig. 8.5. One-piece fiberglass shower enclosure with glass sliding doors. No plastic, please.

Fig. 8.6. Deep utility sink with metal faucet and tile backsplash. No plastic, please

common in manufactured homes. It is the same material that the toilet is made of.

3. Larger mirror over washbasins with a strip light over each. You'll need the extra light.

4. Fiberglass 1-piece tub/shower combo. Porcelain and steel tubs are not available in manufactured homes. Fiberglass can be fine, but avoid plastic tubs and plastic 2-piece shower stalls or tub/shower combinations. The plastic is hard to clean and tends to crack.

5. Tile backsplash

6. If extra storage, such as a linen closet, is offered, get it. It'll come in very handy.

All bedrooms

1. Overhead ceiling light. Yes, many times you have to add them. No plastic light covers.

2. Windows appropriately placed to allow for a headboard. Make sure windows are not "floating" in the middle of a wall.

3. Closets. Make sure they are big enough for you. Have them enlarged if they are too small.

4. Locking door knobs.

Dining room

1. Sheet vinyl ("Linoleum") in dining room. Please order it, certainly if you have kids.

Living room, family room

1. Windows appropriately located, depending on placement of your furniture.

2.   Overhead ceiling lights, if you want them. It's very expensive to add them later and you can cover the boxes with a fascia if you decide not to use them.

Entry way

1.   Sheet vinyl ("Linoleum") in entry by front door. By all means get it. You will save carpet life.

All rooms

1.   No heat vents in traffic areas (if there are, the factory can move them. Also look around the island in the kitchen. A heat vent will be bent beyond being fixed here. Check where you are going to put your bed. Is there a heat vent right under it? What about living areas? Are there any vents right in the middle of the room? This minor detail makes a huge difference in how you enjoy your home.

2.   30-inch interior doors where possible.

3.   Metal mini blinds.

Recommended Options

Here is a list of options to seriously consider if they are within your budget:

1.   4:12 pitch roof (meaning 4 inches of rise per horizontal foot). Most manufactured homes come with a nominal 3:12 pitch and the problems you can run into with such a slight pitch are twofold. Number one, the rainwater and melting snow won't run off the roof at a substantial speed, so when the water gets to the edge of the shingles it goes around the edge of the shingles then back up the backside. This reduces the life of your roof. Number two, the roof decking will get wet from the water going under the shingles. Besides, the steeper pitch makes your manufactured home look more like a house.

2. Vinyl siding. Since I'm an advocate of low maintenance , I'm all for lifetime, no painting siding. The hardboard siding is better than it used to be, but it's still not that great. Besides, manufacturers tend to hide flaws caused by the fastener nails with putty, which can make your house look like a "connect the dots game." Make sure the vinyl siding is attached to a ⅜-inch backer that has first been attached to the house. If it doesn't have a backer, order it or buy something else.

3. Cement lap siding. It has a 50-year warranty. Make sure you are satisfied with how the manufacturer applies this product to the house.

4. Recessed entry. You want to get out of the rain, right? It's also more residential looking.

5. 30 lb. roof load. Depending on where you live, a 20 lb. roof load may work. If you live where it snows a lot, get an 80 lb. roof load. Personally, a 30 lb. would be minimum for me.

Fig. 8.7 and 8.8. Roof pitch compared. The single-wide on the left has a standard 3:12 pitch, while the home on the right has a 4:12 pitch.

6.   French doors instead of sliding patio doors. They don't have the inherent problems of sliding glass doors.

7.   Built-on dormer. This is the peak or gable that is built on the roof. It breaks up the flat roof line and gives angles to your home. Make sure it is placed so a valley or channel is not created over the front door. A raging waterfall over your head is for vacations only.

8.   Aluminum covered eaves and fascia.

9.   Foundation-ready chassis. This option is necessary only if the home will be set on a solid poured perimeter foundation or a basement.

Kitchen

1.   Stove upgraded one step. You'll enjoy the timer and clock. You may want to take the credit for this appliance and buy your own. Just add the price of what you want to install to the price of the house.

Fig. 8.9. Six-panel interior door.

Fig. 8.10. French patio doors are preferable to standard sliding doors.

2.   A larger refrigerator than the standard (18 cu. ft. minimum). Gives you more room and it and can accommodate an ice maker.

3.   A built-in microwave. Since manufactured house kitchens can be short of kitchen counter space, have a built-in microwave put in over the stove.

4.   A deep stainless steel sink. Porcelain sinks can crack if you drop a skillet on them. Make sure the sink is at least 8" deep—any less and the sink will hardly hold a plate and a cup.

11.   An extra bank of drawers. One bank of four or five drawers is not enough. Order at least one more for storage.

Utility room

1.   A gas furnace and gas water heater. They are generally better products than their electric counterparts. If you have access to gas, get them. Gas water heaters have quicker recovery and are cheaper to operate.

2.   Large utility sink. No plastic.

Dormer over the home's entry and living area to add interest to the roof line.

Master bath

1.   Two washbasins with a mirror and strip light over each helps with resale.

2.   Separate stall shower (make sure it's one-piece fiberglass)

3.   Medicine cabinet

4.   Bank of drawers

Guest bath

1.   Medicine cabinet

2.   Bank of drawers

Master bedroom

1.   Cathedral ceiling

All rooms

1.   Painted, solid wood door molding. Commonly used is a particle board product wrapped with a paper or vinyl material. The vinyl can pull away from the molding, and if there is a smoker in the house, it can discolor.

2   Rounded corners. This softens the look and feel of your house.

3.   4- or 6-panel doors. They are heavier than standard hollow-core doors and have better hinges. They should be full length (not 2 inches short of the floor).

4.   Baseboard molding. These are more residential looking and protect walls when you vacuum.

5.   Insulated interior walls for sound and heat.

6.   Single-lever door handles

7.   Tape and texture, at least in the living areas.

Living room

1.   Wiring for ceiling fan

Other Options

Here's a list of options you may want to purchase outside of the factory:

Kitchen

1.   Appliances

Master bath

1.   Towel bar and tissue holders

Electrical

1.   Ceiling fan

2.   A better thermostat, such as a Honeywell. Many homes come with a plastic thermostat.

Guest bath

2.   Towel bar and tissue holder

Living room

1.   Wood or pellet stove

2.   Valances

Unnecessary Factory Options

Here is a list of options the manufacturer may offer but which you should avoid.

1.   Skylights. The plastic ones tend to turn cloudy. The glass ones are better but, like the plastic ones, can eventually leak.

2.   Swamp coolers. Please don't cut a hole in your roof. In time it will leak. Besides, a swamp cooler on your roof makes your home look like a trailer.

3.   Ceiling fans. Buy one at a hardware store for less and get a choice of styles.

4.   Telephone and TV jacks. Have these installed by a professional outside of the factory. Chances are good if you do have the factory install them they will be in the wrong spot.

5.   Storm doors. Manufacturers offer cheap doors. Don't buy them.

6.   Towel bar and toilet paper holders. Buy them for less and get nicer ones at a hardware store.

7.   Outswing doors. Avoid them. You will lose heat and energy.

8.   No metal roof or siding. It's no fun sealing your roof or waxing the siding every fall, nor is it attractive to put tires on the roof to prevent the metal from flapping in the wind.

9.   Wood stoves, pellet stoves, fireplaces. I recommend you purchase none of these from the factory. The wood stove selection is limited and the hearth is mediocre at best. The same thing goes for the pellet stove. Forget the fireplace completely: it'll be cheap and cheesy, not to mention the heating inefficiency. Wood stoves and pellet stoves are a terrific way to heat your house; but have a professional install your choice of stove and vent it out a wall. Avoid cutting any holes in the roof.

10. Log siding, cedar siding. It's a nice idea, but do you really want to treat your siding every year? Plus the rust stains running down your house from the nails used to apply the siding just don't look good.

11. Fancy dining room chandelier. Have the home wired for one only, then get your own at a hardware store. It will be cheaper and you'll have a wide selection to choose from.

Let me summarize the different ways to option your home:

1. Take the credit on the option; get a cost on its replacement and add it to the price of the home.

2. Take the option that's standard in the home and then change it later or sell it yourself.

Now that you have an idea as to how I recommend you option your home, let me tell you why. In the early to mid 1990s, the cost of lumber and options to put in your home was reasonable. Then, many dealers were hit with lumber surcharges and option cost increases. The same home cost $5–6,000 more in 1997 than it did in 1994.

What I see many dealers doing to cut their cost and reduce the selling price of a home is show their display homes with flash—the home on display may have vinyl siding and a 4:12 pitch roof to catch your eye—but inside the home is "stripped." It may have plastic sinks, fixtures, and hardware and while it may still have vinyl-clad energy-

Fig. 8.11. A nice deck with steps and a walkway. The deck is high due to the sloping ground.

efficient windows, it may have only 2 x 4 exterior walls with minimal insulation, perhaps with a R-11 rating.

It is important to have 2 x 6 exterior walls with R-21 insulation. The dealer may have cut down on the ceiling insulation too.

There are many more examples of this, but you get the idea. It is best to order you home with the options you want, don't fall for a sell job on a dealer stock home unless you have seen the option sheet and it has all that you want in the way of options and upgrades.

Other "Bits and Pieces"

I need to drive this point home, so I am going to say this as plainly as I can. Do *not* take the standard carpet or be talked into buying the manufacturer's so-called "upgrade" carpet. None of it will last more than a few years. Someday, maybe, this will change, but for now, your best deal will be to go to a carpet store and buy at least 52-ounce carpet. The carpet pad needs to be at least a 6-pound pad—the thickness doesn't necessarily matter. If your pocket book allows, 7-pound pad would be even better.

Salespeople do not understand most of this process, so you have to. Many times a factory spec sheet will show a 30-gallon water heater standard and then an optional 40-gallon water heater for $95.00. The 40 gallon water heater does not cost just $95.00. The $95.00 is added to the cost of the 30-gallon water heater that is already standard in the house.

Kitchen appliances work the same way. The dealer says that the standard stove that comes in your home can be upgraded for $65.00, right? The stove probably cost the factory $220.00. The factory in turn makes a profit on the stove by charging the dealer $320.00. The $65.00 upgrade stove will have a clock and timer that you would like. Who wouldn't? So your total charge is $385.00. Go to Sears. The same stove is probably much less.

Concerning electrical wiring, you want copper and a 4-wire system. I understand site-built homes are being converted to this. You can expect the following gauges to be used in your home: 12-2 in the kitchen, a 12-3 with ground, 14-2 for lighting circuits (the first number is the gauge, or thickness—the lower the number, the thicker the wire—and the second number stands for how many wires). No more fire traps.

Have any wood parquet flooring installed after delivery and set-up of your home. The shifting from transport can make a real mess. Also, oak entries can take a beating and can fade and crack with use.

IMPORTANT HEALTH NOTICE

Some of the building materials used in this home emit formaldehyde. Eye, nose, and throat irritation, headache, nausea, and a variety of asthma-like symptoms, including shortness of breath, have been reported as a result of formaldehyde exposure. Elderly persons and young children, as well as anyone with a history of asthma, allergies, or lung problems, may be at greater risk. Research is continuing on the possible long-term effects of exposure to formaldehyde.

Reduced ventilation resulting from energy efficiency standards may allow formaldehyde and other contaminants to accumulate in the indoor air. Additional ventilation to dilute the indoor air may be obtained from a passive or mechanical ventilation system offered by the manufacturer. Consult your dealer for information about the ventilation options offered with this home.

High indoor temperatures and humidity raise formaldehyde levels. When a home is to be located in areas subject to extreme summer temperatures, an air-conditioning system can be used to control indoor temperature levels. Check the comfort cooling certificate to determine if this home has been equipped or designed for the installation of an air-conditioning system.

If you have any questions regarding the health effects of formaldehyde, consult your doctor or local health department.

Wheelchair Access

Manufactured homes can be handicapped conducive. Here is what to do. Order the widest interior doors possible to get a wheelchair through. If you need a higher toilet, you will probably need to have it installed as a replacement after the house is delivered. Grab bars for the shower and toilet areas should be installed at the factory to be covered by warranty. You will need to measure heights and other dimensions for the assembly line to properly place them.

Information on Formaldehyde

Some people notice a distinct odor upon entering a new manufactured home. It is a blend of new construction materials and formaldehyde. Some people are very sensitive to it and others aren't. My experience has been that after a few months the smell dissipates and is unnoticeable. However, some people experience burning eyes and lungs. Energy-efficient homes will hold air in so well, that sometimes mechanical venting is required to adequately ventilate. In addition, crack some windows. Above is a copy of a health notice required by law to be displayed in every home set up for viewing on a dealer's lot.

The Energy-Efficient Home

IF YOU live in the Pacific Northwest, "Super Good Cents" will be a familiar term: it's a measure of the home's insulation quality. In areas with less severe weather, heavy insulation isn't as much a necessity. However, in the Southwest, where air conditioners are common, it is a good idea to have a well-insulated home with dual pane windows. Here is how the Super Good Cents program came into existence in the Northwest.

Around 1990, Bonneville Power got together with manufactured home companies and agreed on a deal in which, if the factories would produce an energy-efficient home with an electric furnace, Bonneville Power would send a $3,500.00 rebate, in cash, to the home buyer. This was designed to help Bonneville Power sell more electricity. It also put some money back into the home buyer's pocket.

The manufactured home companies thus began to produce a "new mobile home." This one had 2 x 6 exterior walls, 2 x 6 floor joists, and real engineered trusses. It also had dual-pane, vinyl-clad windows. Then came the insulation. Manufacturers began to increase the R-values (which is a measurement of insulation and its effectiveness—the higher the number, the better).

This program became extremely successful, and production of manufactured homes increased dramatically. Demand increased each year, costing Bonneville Power millions of dollars, which motivated Bonneville Power to reduce the rebate to $2,500.00. Also, the rebate was taken out of the home buyer's hands and sent to the manufacturer. Still, orders increased and manufactured homes' popularity kept growing.

Finally, the $2,500.00 rebate was reduced to $1,500.00 and then completely dropped in 1995. Depending on where you live, there may have been a program similar to this with similar rebates.

During the boom years of the Super Good Cents rebates, a few misconceptions were spawned that I would like to correct for you to help with an informed buying decision:

1. You can buy a Super Good Cents home with 2 x 4 exterior walls.

2. You can purchase a Super Good Cents home that can be all gas as long as the furnace is electric.

3. The minimum R-value for a Super Good Cents home is 22 for the floor, 33 for the ceiling, and 19 for the walls.

4. A Super Good Cents home can have only a limited amount of glazing (window area).

5. You don't have to have argon gas between the panes of glass in the windows to be a Super Good Cents home.

Although Bonneville Power does not have a rebate anymore, you should check with your local power company. They may have a rebate program of their own for energy-efficient homes, or they may give initial discounts for hookup. Competition among manufacturers has become extremely aggressive, so many dealers will advertise higher R-values, argon gas filled windows, and other energy saving features. They will also charge you accordingly.

If the dealer offers a Super Good Cents home with vinyl-clad windows optional, don't buy it, because vinyl-clad windows should be standard in all homes. Also, don't let them sell you argon gas-filled windows unless they're standard. Initially, the gas will improve the insulation factor by about 2 points, but after a few years, the argon will leak out.

Finally, low-E glass. This is a film between the two panes of glass. It will act as an ultraviolet radiation buffer which will result in fewer fade marks on your furniture and your carpet. Here is the difference. Clear glass windows have a .45 U-value. Low-e windows will have a U-value of .37. The lower U-value, the better. Super Good Cents homes are extremely energy-efficient and I do recommend them or something equivalent.

You may or may not be versed in building codes and what they mean, but you should know the meaning of the R- and U-values. The U-value is a number that expresses the house's overall energy rating. The smaller the number the better. Did you know that Oregon's site-built house U-value is .060, while super good cents is .054? That's 10 percent better—not bad, huh?

The R-value is a measure of the insulation quality of a particular insulating material, and it's really a function of its thickness. The higher the number, the better the insulation quality. Super Good Cents numbers are as follows:

□ R-33 ceiling insulation

□ R-49 for ceiling in flat-ceiling triple-wides

□ R-19 wall insulation

□ R-22 floor insulation

□ .37 NFRC-rated dual pane, vinyl clad windows with low-E glass.

□ There also are extra gaskets around electric wall outlets and so forth.

□ The heat crossover duct will have a minimum R-rating, too.

10.

Be Your Own Contractor

IN THIS chapter, I'll show you how to be your own general contractor and save money. This is another step in being in control of your home buying process. It's not as hard as you may think. Dealers love to keep a tight rein on this process, because many like to kick a little extra profit in the costs of your improvements. It doesn't matter if you're doing a land-home project or putting a single-wide in a park. Overseeing this process will prevent heartache and an empty wallet.

Be prepared for certain new challenges to arise and a great many details to cover, but you will find contractors and building inspectors that are willing to work with you if you follow a logical process. The following pages will give you a step-by-step list to follow.

There will be deviations from time to time, but this is normal. Every one is different but if you follow this systematic procedure, you'll be prepared for those too.

Putting a Home in a Park

Follow these simple steps if you are putting a home in a park. You may have to fall out of sequence from time to time, but this will give you the starting points. It will be worthwhile—remember, many dealers who tell you they arrange your improvements mark them up with or without a contractor's knowledge to make more profit for themselves.

1. Secure financing. Reread Chapter 4, dealing with financing, if necessary. This may be the only time to finance at the dealership—but try a mortgage company first.

2. Go and inspect manufactured home parks, get their monthly rent and a list of covenants.

3. Select the home that best suits your needs.

4. Get the dimensions of the home.

5. Go back home and call a skirting company and get a bid. Make sure it is vinyl skirting with a lifetime warrantee and that it has venting. I would advise against skirting that is made to look like "river rock," because it can warp and buckle due to temperature changes.

6. Call and get bids on the improvements you would like—decks, garage, awnings, gutters, air-conditioning. Get at least two bids on everything.

7. Get the bids in writing and take them to the bank or dealership, depending on where you are financing.

8. The contract to purchase should have these improvements written on it with the cost next to them. Make sure the home price is written separate from the improvement costs.

9. Write it up. After negotiation of course.

10. If you are taking deliver of a home from the dealer's stock, agree upon a move-in date and put it in the contract.

11. If you are ordering a home from the factory, agree upon a move-in date and put it in the contract.

12. Make sure to keep the original bids for improvements.

13. Make sure improvements are done to your satisfaction.

14. Once the house arrives and is set up, go through the home with the option sheet and make sure everything you paid for is there. If it is not, make the dealer correct the situation. The option sheet is considered a part of the contract to purchase.

Putting a Home on Your Own Land

If you are starting with bare land with no improvements, or if you are able to hook to the city sewer and water, you will have a bigger undertaking. Take a breath. It can be fun.

1. Secure financing. Reread the chapter on financing if necessary. *Don't* finance at a dealership.

2. Go and shop for your favorite house. See the chapter on price and negotiation. Write it up.

3. Get the dimensions of the house.

4. Look at land with a realtor.

5. Go home and call the contractors. Get at least two bids per improvement. Here are some possible improvements you may need for bare land:

   ◻ Foundation

   ◻ Well

   ◻ Septic tank

   ◻ Power

   ◻ Gas

   ◻ Driveway

   ◻ Garage

6. If you are within reach of city sewer and water, get bids to hook up from the city.

7. Apply for a building permit at the building department, taking along a copy of the contract to purchase for your home.

8. Once you have a permit, have the contractor do a perk test. This can take several days, so start early.

9. If you are ordering your home, find out the time frame of delivery.

10. Have your road built first, if you need one.

11. Then the foundation should be built.

12. Then the well should be dug, and the septic tank put in place.

13. The garage comes next.

14. Make sure a representative from the dealership comes to plan the best way to bring the house onto your site.

15. Home delivered.

16. A final inspection will be done by an appraiser and sent to the bank for final review. This is referred to as a "442."

17. The bank will draw up closing documents and send them to a title company.

18. The title company will call you and set up a time for you to close your loan.

19. Once the closing is done, the title company will disperse funds to the dealer, contractors, or any other parties involved.

A Note on Deposits

When it comes time to sign a purchase agreement, the salesman will ask you for a certain amount of down payment. Many times, the dealer will tell you they need 5 or 10 percent of the purchase price of the home to order it from the factory. Dealers like to blame this on the factory. You may hear, "The factory has to have this money to begin production of your home."

This isn't true. It's just one way of getting money out of you. Wouldn't you prefer to hold on to your money, earning interest, as long as possible?

Here's what you do: Since you've already been approved at a bank or by a mortgage company, you know what your down payment will be, and that is what you bring to closing at the title company. Do not give it to the dealership. Give them $100–200, tops. Tell them you will have your bank send them a commitment letter. The dealer will get all his money at closing. Don't let them buffalo you. If they refuse to order the home without a huge amount of money, tell them it's your way or no way. They may frown and squirm, but they need your business. If they still give you a hard time, take your business elsewhere. This industry has become so competitive, you will find a dealer to do it your way.

Let me give you a scenario that happened when a home buyer gave the dealer too much money. Everything seemed to be in place. Mr. Buyer had an accepted offer on the land. He had bids on improvements. He had a home picked out and unfortunately let the nice salesman talk him into giving the dealership $20,000.00. Then he went and got financing at a bank. The home was perfect and Mrs. Buyer was happy. The problem arose when they wanted to start improvements on the land.

The land seller wanted to be paid in full before anyone ever touched his property. The banker wasn't aware of this and did not structure the loan to be staged (meaning there would be a closing on the land and then another one on the house and improvements). The cost of the land was $15,000.00 and all Mrs. Buyer's money was where? At the dealership. Mr. Buyer asked the dealer to give some of the money back so he could pay off the land seller. Of course the dealer said, "No." How shocking.

What did Mr. Buyer have to do? He had to grovel to the land seller to take $10,000.00 (he got from his IRA) and a note payable for $5,000.00 in 60 days. This process took an additional 30 days. No help from the dealer and no help from the bank. You see the importance of the sequence of steps that I gave you.

11.

Materials and Construction

IT IS important to be aware of the types of materials used in your house and how those materials react together in a finished product. In this chapter, I have put together a smattering of areas for you to think about. Remember that I am not an engineer or a contractor. My point of view is from experience and from talking to set-up crews in the field. Also remember that manufactured homes are built differently than site-built homes. Because of the code that manufactured homes are built to, some of the building materials can be of lesser quality. You must be the final judge. Let's start at the top and work down.

Roof

The Uniform Building Code for site-built homes says that there must be "felt" (felt paper—a water barrier) applied to the roof decking before the shingles are attached. Manufactured homes may or may not have some type of "felt."

The trusses that support the roof are 2 x 2 or smaller on a factory-built house with a 3:12 pitch roof. If you order a 4:12 roof, the manufacturer may automatically use a 2 x 3 or a 2 x 4 truss, but you will have to ask. Site-built homes generally have 2 x 6 trusses or the increasingly popular "I-joist."

Exterior Walls

Siding is also something to consider. As I have mentioned before, my choice would be vinyl siding or something similar that requires no painting. If you choose hardboard, be prepared to paint and replace.

Hardboard siding is a wood-based material that is made by binding wood fibers together under pressure. If the siding should become damaged, repairs need to be made quickly. Some type of sealer that matches the paint should be used. If you don't make repairs, water will infiltrate the siding, causing it to swell. I don't recommend using nails or screws to attach anything to your siding, because they create holes through which moisture could penetrate and do serious damage.

Hardboard and wood siding materials differ. Some manufacturers use wood cedar shingles which I do not recommend. They change color from red to grey and you will have to stain them every year or so.

Caulking is very prevalent with hardboard siding. This is done to keep moisture from getting behind trim around windows, etc. Caulking can become brittle and it can collect dirt and oil from the air. You will have to inspect the caulking every year, and you usually have to replace some of it. I hope this explains why I recommend vinyl siding.

Take into account the fact that many manufacturers do not use a wind barrier before the siding is applied. Tyvek or some other brand is used on site-built houses. Older site-builts may not have a wind barrier, but all newer homes should have it. Again, do not accept a factory-built home that does not put some type of backer, that is 4 x 8 sheets of plywood or oriented strand board on first before the vinyl siding is attached.

Moving inside, site-built homes use $\frac{3}{8}$ to $\frac{1}{2}$ inch sheetrock. I have yet to see a manufactured home with more than $\frac{1}{2}$ inch. If your budget allows, stay away from that thin $\frac{3}{8}$-inch sheetrock with wallpaper. It is very thin, and if a hole or blemish occurs on one of the walls, you'd have to replace the entire panel. Besides, the particular wallpaper has probably been discontinued by the manufacturer, leaving you in a bind with no way to match the patter.

Next, compare how the sheetrock is attached to the wall studs. site-built homes will use drywall screws and many manufactured homes do, too. However, some will use foam with a chemical reaction to bond the sheetrock to the studs. My experience with homes in the field has been fair at best with this process. The foam tends to squeeze between the stud and the sheetrock, making a bulge appear along the stud line. Maybe someday the technique will be perfected, but for now it makes for an uneven wall and ceiling.

Does the manufactured home you are considering have taped corners? By this, I mean the joint where the wall meets the ceiling and wall meets wall. Are the corners taped and then textured? Or is there a thin bead of caulking running down this very important joint? The caulk will dry and become brittle and can pull away. This won't look good, and you'll have to caulk again and again.

Floor and Substructure

Most site-built homes have plywood floor decking. That's the wood you walk on. It can be ¾ inch thick or more. In a manufactured house, floor decking is typically a type of particle board and is ½ to ¾ of an inch thick. It is applied in 6 x 14 or 8 x 14 sheets and is held in by nails or sometimes screws. Some manufacturers use 4 x 8 sheets of tongue-in-groove oriented strand board. The potential problem with mobile home decking is that when the exterior walls are set down and fastened to the floor, it puts a tremendous amount of weight on the perimeter of the floor deck and can make the decking rise in the middle. This is called "crowning."

There are different sizes of floor joists available, 2 x 4, 2 x 6, and 2 x 8 inches. The 2 x 6 works fine; however, the 2 x 8 is twice as strong. I do not recommend the 2 x 4-inch floor joists.

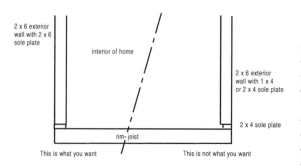

2 x 6 exterior wall with 2 x 6 sole plate

interior of home

2 x 6 exterior wall with 1 x 4 or 2 x 4 sole plate

2 x 4 sole plate

rim-joist

This is what you want

This is not what you want

Fig. 11.1. Comparing a 2 x 6 soleplate used with 2 x 6 walls with a narrower 1 x 4 (or a 2 x 4) sole plate. Although the narrower sole plate is not a code violation, it's not satisfactory. Insist on a 2 x 6 sole plate.

A lot of manufacturers use a 1 x 4 sole plate (the bottom framing of the exterior walls). You should make sure you get one that is 2 x 6, instead; otherwise you can't attach baseboard in the home.

The Heating System

Another major difference between manufactured and site-built homes is the heating system. First, the furnace itself will be different. In the Northwest, the two big suppliers to factories are Coleman and Intertherm. These products are okay, but definitely not top of the line. The efficiency of gas and electric heaters is about 80%. You can get the BTU (British Thermal Units) for gas and kW (Kilowatts) for electric ratings of the units installed.

Many manufacturers put the same size furnace in all of their models, regardless of the number of square feet in the house. It seems to make sense that a 2,500 sq. ft. triple-wide would require a larger furnace than a 900 sq. ft. single-wide. For larger double- and triple-section homes, I recommend ordering a furnace that is larger than the manufacturer's standard furnace. Make sure the right model is installed initially.

Most manufactured homes also give you a one-size-fits-all heating duct system built into the floor of your home. This means that the duct is

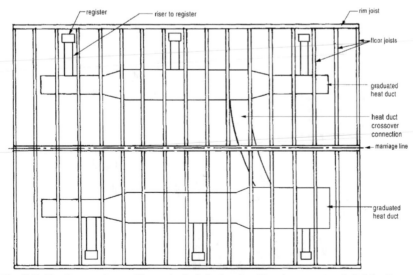

Fig. 11.2. Heating system with graduated ducts, resulting in even heat distribution. The registers are along the outside walls, away from the traffic pattern.

the same dimension the entire length of your house. My experience with living in a factory-built house with this system is that your utility room, where the furnace is, will be very warm, while the master bathroom will be cold. Here's the reason: As the air comes out of the bottom of the furnace into the head duct, it loses speed as it travels to the other end of the house. It loses speed because the heat duct does not narrow to keep the same volume of air blowing into each room. Thus, the far end of the home will be cooler. To allow the same air speeds, you need a graduated heat duct system, which maintains the same volume of air in every room.

Condensation and Ventilation

This are problems all manufacturers are concerned about. It may seem odd, but the more energy-efficient and tightly constructed a home is, the more condensation problems it can have. Condensation is the process of vapor (all air contains vaporized water) changing from the gaseous to the liquid state. Warm air absorbs evaporated water much like a sponge. As this warm air gets into contact with colder surfaces, such as exterior windows, walls, and water pipes, it can hold less moisture. Cooling warm air is like squeezing a wet sponge: the moisture comes out, and it collects on your windows and on many other surfaces in your home.

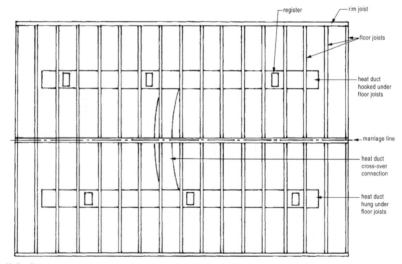

Fig. 11.3. Conventional "one-size-fits-all" heating ducts, resulting in poor heat distribution and registers poorly placed in the traffic areas.

Examples of activities that cause additional water vapor are drying clothes, cooking, bathing, dishwashing, and using gas appliances. However, the biggest contributor of water vapor in your home will be you yourself, by inhalation and perspiration.

Make sure to read your homeowner's manual about how to control condensation. Methods used to control the problem can include exhaust fans, avoiding or reducing use of humidifiers, and cracking windows.

Manufacturers can reduce the problems using two methods: mechanical and passive. Passive venting uses strategically placed vents under the eaves, on the ends of the house, and on the roof.

Mechanical venting exchanges air with the outside fresh air by pressurizing the attic cavity and keeps the air circulating. If you see a manufactured home with little or no venting under the eaves, there is a good chance the home is mechanically vented by a fan somewhere in the attic cavity. The fan is designed to run day and night, 365 days a year.

The advantage of passive venting is that you don't have to worry about mechanical breakdown. It is also silent and energy-efficient.

If your home is set on a foundation, or is skirted for that matter, there are always vents installed under the house to allow air to circulate freely underneath, allowing it to breathe. A mechanical device is not required.

Consumer Reports Survey

Since it is available, let me give you some information from *Consumer Reports*, February 1998. What it tells us is some of the major items of concern with manufactured homes that agree with items listed here in this book. Its findings after surveying 1,029 consumers nationally include:

1.   Manufactured housing can last as long as site-built housing. As with many things, the more expensive the house, the fewer problems you are likely to have.

2.   Eighty-two percent of the respondents were largely satisfied with their manufactured home. A majority had at least one major problem.

3.   Owners of homes placed in mobile home parks felt vulnerable to landlords who had the power to increase space rent.

4.   HUD has been a major factor in raising standards of quality in manufactured housing.

The major weak spots the respondents identified were floors, central heating and cooling, plumbing, roofing, windows, doors, and installation. Let's look at each one.

Floors	One fourth of those surveyed had problems with the particle board flooring. It can swell if it gets wet and breaks down.
Central heating and air conditioning	Improper placement of registers resulted in uneven heating and cooling. One fifth reported having problems.
Plumbing	Polybutylene pipes may leak. Manufacturers are dropping this product and other cheap plastic piping, but check anyway. Thirty-six percent had problems with plumbing.
Roof	Thirty-one percent of those surveyed had problems with their metal roofs leaking at the seams. These roofs are not so common in the Northwest, but many are sold elsewhere.
Windows and doors	Gaps in door and windows (broken seals) may be the result of transporting the home from factory to site. Windows of lesser quality have their corners joined with fasteners, not a continuous weld. They leak. Thirty-two percent of purchasers had to deal with leaking windows.
Installation	Homes not set on a poured concrete foundation are more susceptible to cracking tape and texture and sticking doors and windows.

Consumer Reports did an excellent job, and I do suggest you read the article.

Worksheets and Option Lists

H ERE ARE some useful worksheets and quick lists for a manufactured home buyer (take these with you when you go shopping).

Land-Home Package Worksheet

Home + air conditioner + tax . . . .

Land   . . . .

Improvements

     Foundation   . . . .

     Garage   . . . .

     Driveway, misc. concrete   . . . .

     Septic tank   . . . .

     Well . . . .

     Power   . . . .

City sewer and water . . . .

Gas hook-up . . . .

Electric. . . . .

Decks . . . .

Permits . . . .

Miscellaneous . . . .

Total Project Cost . . . .
Down Payment . . . .

Amount to Finance . . . .

Estimated taxes and insurance . . . .

Amount to finance . . . .

Term in years . . . .

Interest rate . . . .

Monthly payment (principal and interest) . . . .

Monthly taxes and insurance . . . .

Monthly PMI if applicable

Monthly Grand Total . . . .

Plan of Action

(Use this as a step-by-step written plan, based on your circumstances. Remember the first thing is financing.)

1. . . . .

2 . . . .

3. . . . .

4. . . . .

5. . . . .

6. . . . .

7. . . . .

8. . . . .

Park, Home-Only Worksheet

Home + air conditioner + tax . . . .

     City sewer and water . . . .

     Gas hook-up . . . .

     Electrical . . . .

     Skirting . . . .

     Decks, steps, fencing . . . .

     Permits , Miscellaneous . . . .

Total Project Cost . . . .
Down Payment . . . .

     Amount to Finance . . . .

     Estimated taxes and insurance . . . .

     Term in years . . . .

     Interest rate . . . .

     Monthly payment (principal and interest) . . . .

     Monthly taxes and insurance . . . .

Monthly Grand Total . . . .

Plan of Action

(Use this as a step-by-step written plan, based on your circumstances. Remember the first thing is financing.)

1. . . . .

2 . . . .

3. . . . .

4. . . . .

5. . . . .

6. . . . .

7. . . . .

8. . . . .

Essential Factory installed Options

Exterior

☐ Minimum of 1 outside water faucet

☐ Widest eaves possible

☐ Super Good Cents insulation package or something comparable

☐ Air conditioner ready

☐ Foundation ready

☐ 30 lb. roof load if it snows at all where you live

Kitchen

☐ Solid wood cabinets

☐ Overhead light in pantry

☐ Extra bank of drawers

☐ Metal single-lever faucet

☐ Tile backsplash (not wood)

- Two fluorescent lights

- Eight-inch deep sink

- Shut-off valves under the sink

- Plumbing for ice maker

- Garbage disposal

Utility Room

- Electric outlet for a freezer

- Cabinets over the washer and dryer

- 40 gallon minimum water heater (50 gallon preferred)

- Gas furnace, if possible

- Gas water heater, if possible

Master Bathroom

- Porcelain or vitreous china sinks (china is what the toilet is made of)

- Metal faucets

- Fiberglass shower (1 piece)

- Large mirror over sinks with strip light

- Tile backsplash

- Fiberglass tub

- Shut-off valves under sink

Guest Bathroom

▢ Porcelain or vitreous china sink

▢ Metal faucets

▢ One piece fiberglass tub/shower combination

▢ Strip light over large mirror

▢ Tile backsplash

▢ Bank of drawers

▢ Shut-off values under sink

▢ Extra storage where possible

All Bedrooms

▢ Overhead ceiling light

▢ Make sure windows are not in the middle of the wall (You do not want your headboard under a window. Have the window moved either toward a corner or toward another wall).

▢ Have closets enlarged if necessary (they can be quite small).

Living room, Family Room, Den

▢ Add windows to suit

▢ Ceiling lights

Dining Room

▢ Consider sheet vinyl ("linoleum") on the floor instead of carpet

Entry Way

▢ Entry sheet vinyl ("linoleum")

▢ Avoid oak parquet; it shifts during transport

Essential Options for All Rooms

▢ Check very carefully the placement of all heat vents. Some end up in traffic patterns or where furniture needs to be placed. Have them moved near the exterior walls.

▢ The best carpet that is offered, or take the credit from the dealer and have your own installed. Find out the total square yards in the house, then get a price on at least a 52-ounce carpet. Then simply have the dealer add the cost to the purchase price of the home.

▢ Minimum carpet pad should be 6-pound (your carpet will last much longer)

▢ Metal roller guides on all drawers

▢ Metal door knobs

Recommended Options (based on your budget)

Exterior

▢ Vinyl siding (lifetime warranty with no painting)

▢ 4:12 pitch roof (the steeper pitch looks more residential)

▢ Recessed entry (better protection from the weather)

▢ Dormer or "peak" on the roof to eliminate the flat look

▢ Lighter color shingles (they last longer regardless of warranty)

▢ Meter base

◻ 200-Amp electric service

◻ Patio door (French door—avoid sliding glass doors)

Kitchen

◻ Upgrade appliances at least one step (more features and more attractive)

◻ Built in microwave over the stove

◻ Adjustable shelves

◻ Extra bank of drawers

Utility Room

◻ Utility sink

◻ Gas water heater (if gas is available)

◻ 36 inch rear door

Master Bathroom

◻ Two sinks

◻ Bank of drawers

Guest Bathroom

◻ Bank of drawers

Living Room, Family Room, Den

◻ Wiring for a ceiling fan

Recommended Options for All Rooms

▫ Baseboard molding (protects wall when vacuuming)

▫ 6-panel doors (they are heavier than the standard ones)

▫ Tape and Texture throughout

▫ Single-lever door handles

▫ Extra storage wherever possible

Options to Avoid

▫ Swamp cooler on the roof (remember, holes in the roof cause leaks)

▫ Ceiling fans (buy them at a local hardware store, instead)

▫ Skylights.

▫ Telephone and TV Jacks

▫ Storm doors

▫ Aluminum windows

▫ Towel bar and tissue holder

▫ $\frac{3}{8}$-inch Sheetrock

▫ "Out-swing" trailer doors

▫ 2 x 4 exterior walls

▫ Plastic light covers

▫ Log siding

▫ Cedar siding

▫ Wood and pellet stoves or fireplaces

13.

Flow Sheets

HERE ARE systematic listings of the order of events in the process of buying a manufactured home. In the first section, we'll look at the process involved when the home is to be placed on your own land, based on a typical case. The second part will deal with the process of placing the home in a park.

Home-Land Package Flow Sheet

1. Go to a bank, credit union, or mortgage company. Go through the loan approval process, so you know exactly how much money you can borrow. It can take up to two weeks. Do this before you go shopping for homes.

2. While waiting for approval, begin to gather bids on the improvements from contractors that come highly recommended.

3. When you have been notified of an approval, go shopping for a home and take the purchase agreement for the home, the purchase agreement for the land and all the bids for the improvements to the lender.

4. The lender will then order an appraisal. Be prepared to part with somewhere around $400.00. Appraisal can take 1 to 3 weeks.

5. During this time, you need to go and check on building permits at the court house. These folks will give you specific instructions regarding what paperwork they need from you and will generally work with you.

6. When the appraisal comes back and is satisfactory to the lender, take a copy of the approval letter to the home dealer and have him order the home.

7. Next, call the contractors and have them start the improvements on your land. Please note: Depending on the program you have qualified for at your lender, and depending on the seller of the land, you may have to close on the land before the seller will allow improvements to start.

8. Stay in close contact with your contractors. As each one completes his respective job, the local building inspector will sign off on each improvement. When the foundation is complete, notify the dealer and have the home delivered.

9. Hopefully, the dealer won't take more than 7–10 working days to finish the house. When all the improvements are complete and the detail work on the home is done, the lender will order a final inspection by the appraiser.

10. Upon completion of the final inspection, a closing date at a title company will be set. This is when you will need to bring any funds in and when you officially become a homeowner.

11. The title company will then send payment to the manufactured home dealer, the contractors, and anyone else due funds.

Important Note

This is a typical scenario. Your particular transaction may have a few differences. This is not science, but rather an art. A land-home package can take 90 days or more.

Home-Only Flow Sheet

Here is a systematic listing of the steps you have to take when buying only the home, without buying land and worrying about the many improvements required.

1. Go to a mortgage broker and go through the approval process. It can take up to two weeks. This way you will know exactly how much money you can borrow. Do this before you go shopping for a home. If you decide to finance at a dealer, ask to see the approval letter to check that the dealer did not "bump up" the interest rate.

2. Once you have loan approval, you can begin shopping for a home.

3. When you find a home and settle on a price, you can have the dealer add the cost of an awning or a deck or skirting to the cost of the home. This is what you will take back to the mortgage company.

    Note: Some dealers will offer to line up skirting and decking, etc. This is fine; however, some dealers will charge more than these improvements actually cost—it is pure profit for them. Take some extra time and get independent bids. You may save money. I recommend when you get a price on the home, get a "delivered and set" price only. You can then go hunting for improvement costs. There are skirting contractors and others in the phone book. Get the bids in writing. Take them to the dealership and have the costs added to the purchase agreement.

4. If you are going to place your home in a park, get an application from the one of your choice. The park management will need to contact the dealer for pertinent information such as home size, utility locations and so on.

5. The mortgage company will need a copy of the purchase agreement on the home and will need to get a copy of the lease agreement from the park.

6. Some dealers will require 5 to 10 percent down before delivery of the home. Make sure you know up front.

7.   The part and the dealer will communicate a time for delivery of your home, and then the decks, skirting, and any other improvement that needs to be done. You also need to follow up on this to make sure communication is adequate.

8.   Upon final inspection, you will sign closing papers at a title company and they will send money due to the dealer, and all other parties involved. Important: this is a typical scenario. Your particular transaction may have a few differences. A home only purchase can take 20 to 45 days.

14.

Warranties

WHAT type of warranty do you have and for how long? Look at the chart and make sure your dealer is in agreement.

Manufacturer warranties the following:
At least one year for:

1. Plumbing fixtures (toilets, sinks, shower stalls, bathtubs, faucets)

2. Light fixtures (porch lights, ceiling and wall mount lights, switches, plug outlets, circuit breakers)

3. Appliances (provided by the manufacturer—refrigerator, stove, cook top, garbage disposal, range, microwave, trash compactor, dishwasher, stereo, furnace, water heater, washer, dryer)

4. Cosmetic defects (scratches on walls, ceilings, doors, cabinets, moldings, counter tops, appliances, plumbing fixtures, stained or damaged window coverings, cracked or broken electrical cover plates, stained or damaged shower door, torn shower curtains, damaged hardware (door knobs, pulls etc.), tile or trim caulking defects, stained or damaged siding, trim, or shutters, torn or damaged screens

5.   Floor coverings (carpet, pad, linoleum, outdoor carpet)

6.   Fans (bath and kitchen exhaust fans and ceiling fans)

7.   Roof structure or rafters (roof rafters, main support beam, insulation, wood roof decline, all support lumber contained within roof)

At least 5 years for:

8.   Exterior and interior walls and ceilings (studs, insulation, framing members, all support lumber contained within the outside and inside walls, ceiling surface materials)

9.   Electrical system (wiring, fittings, connections, fixture boxes, junction boxes, main and sub-panel boxes)

10.   Plumbing system (water pipes, drain pipes, gas and oil pipes, fittings, pipe connections, fixture and appliance connections)

11.   Frame or chassis (tow bar, steel structure beneath floor of home)

The following needs to be in writing on the purchase agreement:

Dealer to warranty:

1.   Set-up of home according to manufacturer's specifications

2.   The service (if done by dealer)

3.   Anything else customer and dealer put in writing

The dealer does have a "shared" responsibility with the manufacturer, but may state in the agreement something like "dealer provides no express or implied warranty." Simply put, it completely releases the dealer from liability should your home be a "lemon." But don't get alarmed; this is typical. It's very similar to buying a new car: the dealer is not responsible for the warranty cost of the car, but the manufacturer is. If you have work done on your vehicle under warranty, the dealer, in turn, bills the manufacturer for the labor and parts. It's the same with manufactured homes.

A dependable, responsible dealer will have his own service department and should be able to attend to you should service needs arise.

My suggestion for the quickest service is to first call the dealer. If they can't get to you in 10 days or less, call the factory service department. They may be able to get to you more quickly.

All the appliances in your home have their own factory warranty. If your refrigerator were to break down, the dealer would call someone in the area who is authorized to work on your brand of appliance. Personally, I'd get the name and number from the dealer and call myself. It's much quicker.

Siding, roof shingles, carpet, and window warranties operate in a similar manner.

Be as thorough as you can when it comes to spelling out who is responsible for warranty work. Dealers and manufacturers are quite notorious for fighting over who is responsible for what. And there you are, waiting in the middle. Spell it out and don't be hesitant to call the manufacturer if the dealer does not respond to your satisfaction.

Something you may want to try is to hold back a certain amount of money from the dealer, say 10–20%. This way, you can inspect the house and determine that it is completed to your liking, and then you pay the rest to the dealer. Some dealers will flat-out refuse this, but it can't hurt to try. If you can't get satisfaction from either party, there are State Administrative Agencies listed in the Appendix, in the back of this book that will help resolve warranty and service disputes.

Checklist

Once your home is finished being set up, your dealer should do a thorough walk-through with you for a sort of "how-to" session and to make sure all finish work is complete. They should have a checklist to draw from that you can use for service needs. Before you move any furniture in, use the following list to check that the home was completed to your satisfaction.

Exterior

1. Are all shingles on the roof accounted for?

2. Is the marriage line of the home sealed with a trim board and painted correctly?

3. Does the bottom trim on the house cover where the foundation meets the bottom of the home?

4. Are there any cracks, chips, or dings in the siding?

5. Is there a vent "flapper" covering the vent for the dryer?

6. Do the front and rear entry doors open, close, and lock smoothly?

Kitchen

1. Place a ball on the counter tops. Does it roll off?

2. Are all the cabinet doors straight?

3. Did you get the right appliances?

4. Check for cuts in the linoleum.

5. Check water pressure in the sink.

6. Do the drawers roll smoothly?

Master Bath

1. Are the sinks and tub and shower scratch free?

2. Does the shower door open and close so it seals properly?

3. Check linoleum, if applicable.

4. Do the drawers roll smoothly?

5. Are the cabinet doors straight?

Guest Bath

1. Are the sinks and tub scratch free?

2. Check linoleum if applicable.

3. Check drawers and cabinet doors.

Bedrooms

1. If you moved the windows, are they in the right location?

Living Rooms, Dining Room, Den

1. Did you get those extra windows you ordered?

Utility Room

1. Check linoleum for cuts.

Electrical

1. Did the ceiling get the wiring for a ceiling fan?

Tape and Texture

1. Check the entire ceiling and walls, including the inside of the closets, for even texture application and that there are no bulges in the sheetrock. You should not see any sheetrock seams.

All Rooms

1.   Are all the outlets and light switches straight?

2.   Are the heat vents in the right places?

3.   Do all the interior doors open properly; do they close smoothly and lock correctly?

4.   Do all the windows open and close smoothly and latch correctly?

5.   Is the carpet free from "waves"?

6.   Has the baseboard been installed?

7.   Are there any gouges on any of the doors?

8.   Is the marriage line of the home even where it joins the sections together?

9.   Are the mini blinds complete and do they function properly?

10.   Do all the interior door moldings meet properly in the corners with a minimum amount of patching compound or caulking?

11.   Do all the doors that are supposed to have locking knobs have them?

You will have to use the option sheet with which the home was ordered and the standard features list to make sure everything you ordered is in the home you purchased.

The home will come with a thick package of information, covering subjects ranging from warranty to maintenance and operation. Read it all very thoroughly. It will save you time when it comes to operating things properly and fixing them in case of minor problems.

15.

Contracts

FOR YOUR protection, please make sure the home dealer puts the following wording on your contract to purchase:

1. Deposits given to dealer by customer are 100 percent refundable anytime except after home is ordered.

2. Price is guaranteed for 120 days.

3. Purchase of home is contingent upon financing.

4. Dealer will facilitate warranty between customer and factory.

5. Dealer will re-level home within one year of delivery.

6. Dealer will provide free tape and texture repair within one year of delivery.

7. Customer retains the right to choose the contractor and any sub-contractor to complete any phase of home set-up including, but not limited to, transport, set-up of home, and/or finish work, tape and texture, carpet installation, and cleaning.

It is important to include all these items, especially the last one. It gives you the right to choose any contractor you want to set up your home. But, please, the person you choose to do any phase needs to be licensed and know what he is doing. Don't hire your uncle because he will do something for you at half price, but doesn't know what he is doing. It will cost you dearly, if you do.

How to Shop and Be in Control

Now that you have gone through the loan process and know how much you can spend and, more importantly, how much you are comfortable spending, you can go shopping. This will not be easy. You will encounter salesmen and dealers that do not care about you and only want one thing—your money. Use the following steps and you will save money. You may or may not have an idea of what brand or floor plan or even what these pretty manufactured homes cost, so stick with this program.

1. Since you have done a land/home worksheet and have been qualified at a bank or some other financial institution, you know right where you stand. Do not give any of this information to a salesperson. When you first get to a dealership and a salesperson asks you, "How can I help you?" how should you respond? Read on.

2. You need to see several houses so tell the salesperson you wish to see 2-, 3-, or 4-bedroom homes, whichever you are in the market for, and you need to have base prices on all of them. If a salesperson asks what kind of payment you're looking for, or what kind of price range you need, tell him or her you haven't gotten that far yet. *Under no circumstances go to a salesperson's office.*

3. Take note of all the houses you are interested in, get floor plans and prices and be on your way. Do not give any information to the salesman or dealer except your first name. Make sure you have all the standard features for each model.

4. Take your time at many dealerships and look at many brands and floor plans. Be polite, but tough. Do not worry about making friends with a salesperson. Be sure to take the "Materials" page.

5. When you have made a decision on a brand and model, the fun begins. Go to the dealership and "spec" out the house you are interested in. Take the "Essential options" worksheet pages with you and "Options to seriously consider" and start checking items off. Have the salesperson give you a delivered and set base price to your site. Then ask for a copy of the options sheet and the base price in writing. Tell the salesperson you need to go home and go over your paperwork. If they won't part with it, say good-bye and walk out.

6. More than likely there is another dealer selling the same products somewhere. Simply walk through the same scenario. You will need to do this two or three times.

7. Do not let the salesman write on your spec sheet. Have him do his own for you.

8. Never tell a dealer what you were quoted elsewhere for the house you are negotiating for.

This last point bears some explaining. Harvey Mackay does that in his book *Swim with the Sharks Without Being Eaten Alive*, in a chapter titled "Calling Mr. Otis."

It's a sales scam very common in the car business. It goes something like this: You have gone to different dealers and negotiated all day, all month. You've finally made a deal, and the salesperson writes it up. He casually asks you what price the other dealers were asking. At this point, flushed with victory, you throw away the most valuable asset you have—information (the other dealers' prices).

"Just one last step," the salesperson says, "the sales manager has to okay the deal." He gets on the intercom and says, "Calling Mr. Otis."

Of course, there is no Mr. Otis. He may be the sales manager, but his name is something else. The sales manager shows up and pulls the salesperson out of the room to let you, the prospect stew a while. The salesperson finally comes back, saying, "Otis won't go for the deal, and then proceeds to retrade it up to exactly the same price the other dealers were asking.

Because you now have too much invested emotionally, and your kids are jumping around, you think if I don't take this deal, I'll have to start all over again.

So what's $5,000 more on a $65,000 house? Just a few more monthly payments? That's $36.69 more per month and $13,208 more in interest over the life of your 30-year mortgage. Don't fall for the Mr. Otis trick.

The Price to Pay

The choice of which home is right for you is a personal one. You have the list of base prices, the list of materials, and the formula for figuring the approximate cost that the dealer paid the factory for the home. Your budget will give you some direction and which dealer you felt the best about comes into play as well.

So how do you deal for the best price? Some dealers will part with a home for cost and some will not. It is your job to find the least amount of profit a dealer will take. Start with an offer of the price you have figured and wait for a reaction. The dealer will come back with a price and then the negotiation begins. Play the game. Go back and forth a few times. Never raise your price more than $200 at a time. If you are unsatisfied, begin to get up and leave. You may or may not be given the deal you want, but that's why there are other dealers. Don't be pressured with, "If I can get the price you want, will you buy today?" Tell them you don't know.

Once a price has been agreed upon, the salesman will ask for a deposit, normally 5 to 10 percent down. Give him only $100 and tell him he'll get an approval letter from your bank. Make sure the contract has the clauses on it that I have spelled out under "Contracts" at the beginning of this chapter.

Also, once you have a base price of the home you want, ask the dealer for the name and phone number for the set-up crew who will be setting your home up. Call them to get their contractor's license number and ask what they charge, based on where your property is located and whether the home will be set on a foundation. The contractor will also need to know the length and width of the home plus whether it is a single-, double-, or triple-wide.

Next, ask for the name of the contractor who will do the tape and texture close-up on the home. Call and tell them where the home will be and the dimensions. Get their estimate.

Now it is time to ask who will install the carpet. Call the carpet dealer with the number of square yards in the house and get an estimate. Remember *no* factory carpet.

If you are going to set your home on blocks and not on a foundation, you will need some type of skirting. Vinyl is the most popular. Call to get an estimate. Again the contractor will need to know where the house is and the length and width.

Tell the dealer you will clean the home yourself once all phases are done. Tell them you want a check made out to you for $100.00. You could reduce the price you pay for the house by $100.00, too.

If the dealer refuses to give you the contractors they use to complete your home, and you are trying to determine the exact dealer cost of the home, you will have to get out the yellow pages and get your own bids. It's up to you to find reputable people yourself. Call for references and take all steps to find out if these contractors do good work. If you find someone to do a set-up phase for your home that the dealer doesn't use, tell the dealer who you do want to use and have the dealer and contractor get together, so they can begin scheduling.

You can even call the freight company who will deliver your house and get an estimate.

Take down these estimates and add them together. Take the total and deduct it from the base price of the house. This process is a lot of work, but can save you thousands. Dealers like to add to these costs for a little extra profit. These profits go into the DVF— the dealer's vacation fund.

Doing all this yourself is time consuming, but will give you the costs of setting up your home. This is a powerful tool in negotiation. Use it.

Quick Materials Checklist
(How is this house built and with what materials?)

Are shingles 20, 25, or 30 year warranty? . . . .

Are they held down with nails or staples? . . . .

How many nails per shingle?. . . . .

Is felt used on the roof decking? . . . .

What size are trusses (2 x 2 , 2 x 3, 2 x 4)? . . . .

How far apart are they? . . . .

How is the attic cavity vented? . . . .

Are the windows continuous-weld and vinyl-clad? . . . .

Is the siding 20-, 25-, or 30-year or lifetime warranted? . . . .

If vinyl siding, is it attached to a $\frac{3}{8}$-inch backer? . . . .

Does the home come with Tyvek house wrap? . . . .

What type of paint, and how many coats,
        is used on the exterior? . . . .

What are the R-values of the insulation?

        Ceiling . . . .

        Wall . . . .

        Floor . . . .

What size are the floor joists (2 x 6, 2 x 8)? . . . .

Do the floor joists run with the floor deck or across it
(Transverse or longitudinal)? . . . .

How thick is the floor decking and what is it? . . . .

How thick is the sheetrock? ½ inch, or $\frac{3}{8}$ inch? . . . .

How is the sheetrock fastened to the studs? . . . .

Are the window sills wood, tape and textured,
or vinyl-wrapped? . . . .

Are the mini blinds metal or plastic? . . . .

What is the standard carpet pad? . . . .
(Get a 6 or 7 pound minimum) . . . .

Are the hinges on the door mortised? . . . .

What are the interior doors made of? . . . .

Are the doorknobs metal or plastic? . . . .

Are the cabinets solid wood? . . . .

Do the cabinets have adjustable shelves? . . . .

How many drawers are there? . . . .

Because you are getting the home you want, with the proper options and built the way you want it to be, don't be surprised at the final cost. Even though you've followed my guidelines and come to an agreement with a dealer, your cost for a 1,700 to 2,000 square foot home could be $70,000. Look at the following comparison chart for "per square foot" estimates.

Feature	Manufactured Home (1,700 Sq. Ft.)	Site-built Home (1,500 Sq. Ft.)
Home	$50,000.00-70,000.00	$125,000.00-150,000.00
Land	$15,000.00-25,000.00 (100 x 100 lot)	80 x 100 lot
2-car garage	$12,000.00-20,000.00	(included)
Foundation	$3,500.00- 6,000.00	(included)
Septic Tank	$1,800.00- 3,000.00	(included)
Power	$800.00- 2,000.00	(included)
Permits	$1,500.00- 2,000.00	(included)
Total	**$84,600.00–128,000.00**	**$125,000.00–150,000.00**

These numbers tell a huge story. Manufactured homes give you the opportunity to own more square feet, more land, and give you a bigger range of total cost—depending on where you live and the deal you make on the house. Ask yourself these questions:

◻ Is the site-built home big enough?

◻ Is it located on a large enough lot?

◻ Is it energy-efficient and built to your satisfaction?

Look at the difference in cost per square feet (including land and improvements).

Manufactured home: $49.00–75.00

Site-built home $83.00–100.00

Your costs could even be lower if you educate yourself and learn that it is okay to negotiate with everyone, including landowners, contractors, and, of course, the dealer. You must take charge of the whole process.

Manufactured homes are incredibly energy-efficient and offer hundreds of floor plans, options and details. Don't let the size of your project intimidate you. You will save money and get a great house.

16.

Arm Yourself

IN THIS final chapter, you'll learn how to arm yourself with Saturday morning sales meeting insights.

8 A.M. Saturday—too early to be up and at work on the weekend, but Saturdays, all salespeople work. Typically, Saturday can be the heaviest shopper day of the week. Thus begins yet another 1-2 hour sales meeting. The general manager and sales manager look grimly at the group of lemmings quietly sipping coffee and munching doughnuts.

"Well," the general manager begins, "we had good traffic through this dealership last week, 46 names I have here in front of me. That's good. But," he draws in a big breath, "where are all the write-ups? Forty-six people came here and we got only thirteen signatures on contracts? Has everyone forgotten the rules here? How about the basics? There wasn't even a deposit taken on three of the deals. I suppose everyone is showing customers more than three homes, too? You know people will just get confused."

The sales staff remains still and quiet. Next it is the sales manager's turn. "I don't get it. We train you with all these techniques to sell, and we get numbers like these. Let's do a quick review and maybe today we can see better results. No customer sees a house without first being brought into your office and qualified. Remember that? You have to find out what you're going to sell them. Next, sell them on the company, the service, our insurance, and finance. Remember, you need to be in control. People don't know what they're seeing. Take control!

Don't forget to turn over. Bring in me or the finance manager to work them. We need better numbers.

In the back of the room sits Bob. He is a quiet, honest man who really wants to do the best job he can for people. He understands that the dealership needs to make a profit, but he is concerned about the pressure he is to apply on home buyers. Shouldn't they be given the facts and then allowed to decide when and where and what to buy? He is also concerned about some of the borderline deceptive ads that are being placed in the paper.

Some say things like "Free rent" or "Abandoned house," and he knows they are just hooks to get the people to call or come in.

The sales manager continues, "Don't give people information over the phone. Just tell them enough to get them into the dealership so we can work 'em face to face. Also, push our insurance harder. It may be more expensive than anywhere else, but they don't know it and we can work it into their house payment. Remember that we make huge profits on that stuff."

Bob's eyes roll. Every week seems to be getting worse. What has happened since his interview with the company? Did something change in management? What has happened to "We are in business to help the customer achieve ownership of a home and to help fulfill their wants and needs with a price they can afford?"

Now the general manager is back. "These grosses need to come up, too! Almost all of them are below the mark that I set. (He is referring to the gross profit on each house sold.) The next house sold," he continues, "better have at least 23% profit or everyone gets a reduced commission. Why do you think we don't post prices on houses? Just give people a ballpark figure and sell a monthly payment. Everyone is a payment buyer. People don't care what the bottom line price is."

"And another thing. Make sure these display homes are locked at all times, especially when you're in a house with an up (a customer). That's the absolute best way to control people. Lock them up! By the way," he says as he turns to the sales manager, "make double sure that there are signs on every house that read, 'All our homes are locked to protect them for their future owner.' We can fool everyone with a line like that," he grins.

The sales manager adds, "Everyone be ready for a test. It will be role playing with each and every one of you to see if you've memorized that list of objections and answers I handed out. There is no customer objection that has to go unanswered if you memorized all those comebacks on that paper." (An objection is a question a customer may have.)

Bob is wondering why he can't answer customer's questions with honest information. Why all the run-around?

The sales manager is rolling now. "Be sure to get people into financing ASAP! It's quick and easy and people don't have to inconvenience themselves by going to a bank. If by chance someone asks about the higher interest rate than a bank might offer, tell them it's because our lenders let them finance their loan closing costs and they can put down as little as 3% of their own money. (He doesn't mention that every deal paid the dealership a kickback from the finance company that added up to thousands in clear profit). Not only is this great for people with hardly any down payment, but folks with savings will fall for it too."

"Okay, let's take a break for five minutes, then get back here. I've got more to talk about."

As Bob refills his coffee cup, he overhears some of his coworkers talking about some of their grosses they hold on some of their sales. "I had a couple come in yesterday looking for something used. You know that 1979 single-wide in back? I sold it for $14,900.00. That was $8,000.00 profit."

"Oh, yeah," the other salesman answered. "That triple-wide I sold—cash in hand buyer—paid the price. He asked me if we give discounts for cash, and I said, 'Of course.' Then I told him a hugely high price on the home and then reduced it. He loved it and we made $19,700.00 on the deal."

Bob is amazed at their willingness to deceive a home buyer to drive up almost $20,000 in profit.

As the sales staff meanders back to the meeting, Bob follows. Okay," the sales manager continues. "Let's talk about the two most important questions to ask someone when they walk through that door. Number one: Have you been here before? Ask this to see if they're shoppers you don't want to waste too much time with. Number two: Do you have a trade? Why do you ask this? So you can quote a higher price on the home they want to buy, then subtract what the customer wants for their trade and you still get the profit on the new home."

"Remember," he continues, "when you sell a trade the profits are huge and your commission can be, too."

"Now, if someone has no land and doesn't want to live in a trailer court, you give them Realty World's card. If they need improvements, like a well or a septic tank ora foundation or a garage, send them to

Coco's Construction. They will do the project and give us a kickback. (Not all contractors give kickbacks, but some do.) "I don't want to hear anyone of you deviate from this plan. It's how we keep total control of customer's projects from start to finish. Now get out there and sell!"

Bob is becoming steadily more perturbed. Since he has a family to support and the possibility of a good income exists here at the dealership, he is stuck with it. Because Bob puts his head down and does the best he can under the circumstances, he decides to tough it out as long as he can, although his conscience hurts him when he thinks of what he's leading his customers into for financing and insurance.

I put this story at the end of the book in hopes of making and reiterating some very important points.

Most salespeople are sincere and want to give good service and sell good products. Many, however, work for dealerships that don't feel this way, and thus the battle between the salespeople and their employer puts you, the buyer, in the middle.

Manufacturers can at times put enormous amounts of pressure on retailers, and many people who operate on the manufacturer's side don't have a clue to the complexity of the retailer's world. I hope this information evens things out a bit and educates dealers , salespeople, factory personnel, and especially you, the consumer, so your learning curve isn't quite so long and confusing. You can learn to drive your project. It doesn't matter if you're buying a single-wide to put in a park or a full-blown land-home package. Spending thousands of dollars entitles you to be in charge, or at the very least, get cooperation from your retailer.

When it comes to price, negotiate hard. Shop and dicker for two or three months, if need be. It's worth your time. Trust your instincts, and if you don't have an instinct, find someone who does and can help you.

This is the American Dream we're talking about here. My hope is that the information here will put you at ease and help you realize that this experience does not need to be a frightening one, but one of excitement and anticipation. Good luck!

Glossary of Terms

ACV
Actual cash value, a term used to describe what a dealer would sell your trade-in for to a wholesaler.

Be backs
Customers who tell salespeople they'll be back.

Bird dogs
People who refer potential home buyers to salespeople for money.

Bumping
Getting a potential customer to raise his offer on a home.

Close
When the home buyer is talked into signing a purchase agreement.

Closer
An employee of the dealership whose only job is to get customers to sign purchase agreements.

Display model
A home which a dealer will display for a model home and then sell in a few months at a "reduced price."

Equity
The value in a home when the payoff is subtracted from the total amount to finance.

Finance charge
The total charges when a customer finances a home, including interest, fees and other charges.

Floor planning or Flooring
When the homes at a dealership are owned by financing institutions rather than the dealer.

Gross back end
Profit a dealer makes on financing and insurance.

Gross front end
Profit a dealer makes on a home sold.

Hard money
Same as ACV

Kickback, Holdback, VIP money
Profit built into each home invoice. It is a percentage of the invoice and is paid to the dealer once a year. This is your money.

PAC	The cost a dealer pays to have a home delivered and set up. Extra profit is sometimes added here.
Payment buyers	Would-be home owners that don't care about bottom line price, only the monthly payment.
Skating	When a salesperson does business with another's customer.
Spiffs	Cash bonuses paid to salespeople for selling a certain model home or achieving a certain amount of write-ups (signed purchase agreements).
T.O.	To turn over a customer to another sales person, sales manager, or closer.
Ups	Customers. Salespeople take turns taking "ups," by watching the front door.
Upside down	If you trade in your home and find you owe more than the house is worth.

Appendix: State Administrative Agencies

Alabama
Manufactured Housing Commission, 906 South Hull St., Montgomery, AL 36130

Arizona
Department of Building and Fire Safety, Office of Manufactured Housing, 1540 West Van Buren Phoenix, AZ 85007

Arkansas
Arkansas Manufactured Home Commission, 523 South Louisiana Street, Suite 500, Lafayette Building, Little Rock, AR 72201

California
Department of Housing and Community Development, Division of Codes and Standards, Manufactured Housing Section, P0 Box 31, Sacramento, CA 95812-0031

Colorado
Housing Division, Department of Local Affairs, 1313 Sherman Street, No. 323, Denver, CO 80203

Florida
Bureau of Mobile Homes and R.V., Division of Motor Vehicles, 2900 Apalachee Pkwy., Room A-129, Tallahassee, FL 32399-0640

Georgia
Manufactured Housing Division, State Fire Marshal*s Office, 2 Martin Luther King, Jr. Drive, Atlanta, GA 30334

Idaho
Buildings Division, Department of Labor and Industrial Services, 277 North Sixth Street, Statehouse Mall, Boise, ID 83720

Indiana
Codes Enforcement Division, Department of Fire Prevention & Building Services, 402 West Washington St., Room W-246, Indianapolis, IN 46204

Iowa
Iowa State Building Code Bureau, Department of Public Safety, Wallace State Office Building, Des Moines, IA 5031 9-0047

Kentucky
Manufactured Housing Division, Department of Housing, Building and Construction, 1047 U.S. 127 South Building, Frankfort, KY 40601

Louisiana
Manufactured Housing Division, State Fire Marshal's Office, 5150 Florida Boulevard, Baton Rouge, LA 70806

Maine
Manufactured Housing Board, Department of Professional and Financial Regulation, State House, Station 35, Augusta, ME 04333

Maryland
Department of Housing and Community Development, Maryland Code Administration, 100 Community Place, Crownsville, MD 21032-2023

Michigan
Manufactured Housing and Land Resources Division, Corporation and Securities Bureau, P0 Box 30222, Lansing, MI 48909

Minnesota
Manufactured Housing Structures Section, Building Codes and Standards Division, Department of Administration, 408 Metro Square Building, St. Paul, MN 55101

Mississippi
Mobile Home Inspection Division, Office of the Fire Marshal, PO Box 22542, Jackson, MS 39205-2542

Missouri
Dept. of Manufactured Housing, R.V. & Modular Units, Public Service Commission, PO Box 360, Jefferson City, MO 65102

Nebraska
Division of Housing and Recreational Vehicles, Department of Health, PO Box 95007, Lincoln, NE 68509-5007

Nevada
Nevada Department of Commerce, Manufactured Housing Division, 2601 E. Sahara Avenue, Suite 259, Las Vegas, NV 89104

New Jersey
Division of Housing and Development, Bureau of Code Services, 3131 Princeton Pike—CN 816, Trenton, NJ 08625-0816

New Mexico
Manufactured Housing Division, Regulation & Licensing Department, 725 St. Michael's Drive, PO Box 25101, Santa Fe, NM 87504

New York
Housing & Building Codes Bureau, Division of Housing and Community Renewal, One Fordham Plaza, Room S-356, Bronx, NY, 10458

North Carolina
Manufactured Housing Division, Department of Insurance, PO Box 26387, Raleigh, NC 27611

Oregon
Building Codes Division, Department of Consumer and Business Services, 1535 Edgewater Drive, NW, Salem, OR 97310

Pennsylvania
Division of Manufactured Housing, Department of Community Affairs, Forum Building, No. 376, Harrisburg, PA 17120

Rhode Island
Building Code Commission, Department of Administration, One Capitol Hill, Providence, RI 02908-5859

South Carolina
SC Department of Labor, Licensing & Regulation, Building & Related Services, 3600 Forest Drive, PO Box 11329, Columbia, SC 29211-1329

South Dakota
Commercial Inspection and Regulation Division, Department of Commerce and Regulation, 118 West Capitol Avenue, Pierre, SD 57501-5070

Tennessee
Manufactured Housing Section, Division of Fire Prevention, 3rd Floor, 500 James Robertson Parkway, Nashville, TN 37243-1160

Texas
Manufactured Housing Division, Department of Licensing and Regulations, PO Box 12157, Capitol Station, Austin, TX 78711

Utah

Division of Occupational and Professional Licensing, Department of Commerce, PO Box 45805, Salt Lake City, UT 84145-0805

Virginia

Manufactured Housing Office, Dept. of Housing & Community Development, Jackson Center, 501 N Second St., Richmond, VA 2321 9-1 321

Washington

Office Of Manufactured Housing, Dept. of Community Trade & Economic Development, PO Box 48300, 906 Columbia St. SW, Olympia, WA 98504-8300

West Virginia

West Virginia Division of Labor, 319 Building Three, Capitol Complex, Charleston, WV 25305

Wisconsin

Manufactured Homes, Safety & Building Division, PO Box 7969, Madison, WI 53707

Index